KU-786-206

Contents

Acknowledgements

Revising this Nutshell book has proved to be a much bigger challenge than I had expected. I wish to express my thanks to a number of people who gave me the support, advice and encouragement which enabled me to complete it. In particular to Ruth, my wife, whose patience and proof-reading skills were enormously valuable. My thanks also go to Rob Hooper, Mary Sutton, Duncan Stoddart and Jeremy Tudway, for their help in reading draft chapters and spotting inconsistencies. I also want to thank Windy Dryden and Alison Poyner for their editorial support and encouragement.

ONE

An Overview of the Person-Centred Approach to Counselling and to Life

An introduction to the approach

When I begin my work with a new client, I usually start by giving them a simple outline of how I work as a person-centred counsellor. In order to try to begin to make my understanding of the person-centred approach more accessible to the reader, I will begin by describing some aspects of how I tell a new client about the way that I work.

Understanding the person-centred approach to counselling can only really come about through connecting the theory to counselling practice, in order to bring it to life. Throughout this book I will be using a number of examples from my client work to try to show how I work as a person-centred counsellor. These casework examples will be composites from my work with a variety of clients, with the individuals' details changed in order to protect confidentiality. None of the examples used will portray any particular individual.

The first meeting with a client

A young woman, Margaret, had been referred to me for counselling by her employer, as she was suffering from stress associated with being harassed by a colleague and was showing some symptoms of depression. When she arrived for her first meeting, I asked her to take a seat and make herself comfortable. I noticed that she sat right on the edge of her chair and was gripping her hands tightly, in a way that seemed rather tense and ill at ease. I introduced myself and told her that I was feeling a little nervous, which I usually do when meeting new people. I then said, in a very accepting way, that she also seemed a little tense and that I suspected she might be feeling a bit nervous or anxious too, at which she nodded quietly in agreement. I asked if she knew anything about counselling, to which she cautiously replied 'No, not a thing'. So I told her that I usually begin by talking a little about the way that I work as a person-centred counsellor, saying something about me and my background and clarifying what we could expect from each other if we agreed to work together. I explained that I believed it was important to do this, so that I could make it feel safe enough for her to talk to me about anything she wanted to. She agreed that this might be helpful and so I began:

'Well, Margaret, there are several different approaches to counselling in this country and I have been trained to work as a person-centred counsellor. There are some important differences between this approach and the other major approaches to counselling.

First, I have a very strong belief in the positive nature of all human beings. We will always strive to do the best for ourselves, no matter what conditions we find ourselves in or what problems we face.

Secondly, I believe in the uniqueness and worth of every individual human being and that we all deserve respect for our capacity to choose our own directions in life and to select and choose our own values to live by.

Thirdly, I believe that you are the only expert in your own internal world and the only person who really knows how you feel. You are the only person who can decide who and how you should be, the only person who can decide what the meaning of your life is and what you should do with it.

Fourthly, I believe that the most important thing in counselling is the therapeutic relationship that will develop between us, in which I hope that you will really feel heard and understood, in a non-judgemental way, and that you will experience me as a real and genuine person in this relationship. I will often be very open with my feelings as I experience

return/renew this item by the last date shown.
may also be renewed by the internet*

brary.eastriding.gov.uk

note a PIN will be required to access this service
be obtained from your library

About the Author

Roger Casemore originally trained as an accountant in local government finance, before reading psychology and then training as a Person-Centred therapist. He began his career in education as a youth worker in London and then progressed to various senior management roles in local authorities and a government quango. He eventually became Director of Continuing Education, Community Liaison, Economic Development, Training and Employment Services, in the Royal Borough of Kensington and Chelsea, until taking early retirement in 1994.

Roger is currently Senior Teaching Fellow and Director of Counselling and Psychotherapy Courses at the University of Warwick. He has practiced privately as a therapist for over 44 years and as a supervisor and trainer of counsellors, for the past 30 years. He is a Chartered Fellow of the Chartered Institute of Personnel and Development and a Fellow of the British Association for Counselling and Psychotherapy. He is a past Chair of the British Association for Counselling, was President of Counselling in Education for 15 years and Chair of the BACP Complaints Committee.

Roger also runs his own consultancy company, Kasmor Consultancy, specialising in organisational development, conflict resolution and conciliation, and the management of cultural change in organisations, in the public, private and not for profit sectors. He also provides a special service of confidential consultancy for chief executives and other senior managers.

Roger has been married to Ruth for 43 years and has two children, Helen and Alastair and two grandchildren, Alice and Sam.

Roger Casemore

Second Edition

PERSON-CENTRED
COUNSELLING
in a nutshell

SAGE

Los Angeles | London | New Delhi
Singapore | Washington DC

OUNSELLING IN A NUTSHELL SERIES Edited By Windy Dryden

SAGE Publications Ltd
1 Oliver's Yard
55 City Road
London EC1Y 1SP

SAGE Publications Inc.
2455 Teller Road
Thousand Oaks, California 91320

SAGE Publications India Pvt Ltd
B-1/I, 1 Mohan Cooperative Industrial Area
Mathura Road
New Delhi 110 044

SAGE Publications Asia-Pacific Pte Ltd
3 Church Street
#10-04 Samsung Hub
Singapore 049483

Library of Congress Control Number: 2010931702

British Library Cataloguing in Publication data

A catalogue record for this book is available from the British Library

ISBN 978-1-84920-734-8
ISBN 978-1-84920-735-5 (pbk)

Typeset by C&M Digitals (P) Ltd, Chennai, India
Printed by Ashford Colour Press Ltd, Gosport, Hants
Printed on paper from sustainable resources

them here, rather than playing the role of counsellor or expert whom you have come to ask for solutions to your problems.

I am not an expert: I do not have any answers to your problems and difficulties. I believe that the answers, if there are any, lie within you. I will not probe or pry into anything you tell me, I will only work with what you choose to talk about. The only questions I will ask will be to check that I have heard and understood your feelings or to clarify the meaning of what you are telling me. I am quite used to a lot of silence, tears and other strong feelings being expressed.

I will be very accepting of what you tell me and, at the same time, I will notice when the words you say seem to be at odds with how I am experiencing you. I might even notice these things out loud, as I did at the start of this session, when I saw that you seemed to be trying to look very calm and in control and yet there were lots of little signals that seemed to suggest to me that you were quite tense. I will do my best not to interpret anything you do or say with my meanings, but I will try to clarify what these things mean for you and how you are really feeling.

I will try to be sensitive in what I say to you and at the same time I would want you to experience me as being really authentic with you and not putting on any pretence. I will be very direct and honest in sharing how I experience you and the things you talk about and you may find this way of working quite challenging at times.

What I will try to do here is to create a trusting relationship between us that will provide a safe space in which I hope you will feel very accepted and understood so that you can be in touch with your feelings and talk, without fear, about anything which concerns you. I have a strong belief that we need to own and value all our feelings, even the most uncomfortable ones, and to be able to say how we feel and to insist on being heard and understood. I hope that you will experience that here with me so that you will feel able to deal more effectively with the feelings that are troubling you.'

That, in a nutshell, is the person-centred approach to counselling.

These words, or something very similar, are the way that I usually start to develop a working relationship with any new client, helping both them and me to settle down and relax and begin to relate to each other. It sounds fairly simple and even rather like common sense, yet I know that to do it well requires considerable knowledge and the expertise that comes from a lot of practice. These words also outline what I believe are the basic principles of the person-centred approach to counselling.

A brief history of the development of the person-centred approach

One of the criticisms of the person-centred approach to counselling is that it is based on very little theory and at times has even been described as 'theory thin'. However, in this book I aim to show that the approach is underpinned by a richness and depth of philosophy and theory, which it is important to understand in order to effectively practise in this way.

Carl Rogers, who was the originator of the person-centred approach to counselling, was born in 1902 in Chicago and died in California in 1987, leaving behind the legacy of what has been called the 'Third Force' in American psychology, namely, humanistic psychology. Rogers was the founder of what he originally called 'non-directive therapy' (Rogers, 1942), which later he changed to calling 'client-centred therapy'. Today it is more popularly known as the person-centred approach. In the late 1940s, at the time that he began to develop his theories, the other two forces prevalent in American psychology were Psychoanalysis and Behaviourism, whose views on human nature were strongly challenged by Rogers.

The development of the person-centred approach stemmed from Rogers' experience of being a client and his experience of working as a counsellor, which gave rise to the views he developed about the Behaviourist and Psychoanalytic approaches to counselling. Rogers felt that, in general terms, the Behaviourists seemed to take the view that human beings are organisms that only react to stimuli, developing habits learned from experience; that individuals are helpless and are not responsible for their own behaviour. The Behaviourists seemed to be saying that individuals have been taught to think and behave in ways that are unhelpful or maladaptive and that it was the counsellor's job to teach them to be different. Rogers also felt that the Psychoanalysts, particularly Freud, appeared to take the view that human beings are never free from the primitive passions originating in their childhood fixations and are solely the product of powerful biological drives. The Psychoanalysts emphasised the dark side of human nature, with its destructive impulses, over which human beings seemed to have no control.

Rogers suggested that in both of these approaches human beings were seen to have no choice and no control over themselves, that individuals are inherently bad or weak, and are likely to get 'broken' and will need the help of the counsellor as an expert who could 'mend' the broken individual. In the process of therapy the counsellor would assess and diagnose what was wrong with the client and identify the goals for change which the client needed to achieve. The counsellor would then direct how the client would achieve these goals by identifying the required strategies the client needed to use in order to resolve their problems.

In his work as a counsellor, Rogers became increasingly uncomfortable with being in the role of 'the expert' and being expected to take a very directive approach to how his clients should change. As a consequence of his experiences as a client in his own therapy and through his contact with other influential psychologists at the time, he began to develop a very different view of human nature and what clients needed to experience in counselling.

I do want to state here that I strongly respect the beliefs and value the good practice of counsellors from the psychodynamic and cognitive-behavioural approaches. I have had good personal experience of therapy from counsellors trained in those approaches. However, I do not feel able to practise those approaches myself because they do not sit well with my personal belief system about the nature of humanity, or with my nature and personality. In simple terms, the person-centred approach seems to fit me and to work well for me and the clients with whom I work.

The basic philosophical assumptions

In my view, Rogers developed the person-centred approach to therapy from three distinctive philosophical beliefs: Humanism, Existentialism and Phenomenology. I believe that in order to understand the theory he developed, it is essential to understand and accept those philosophical roots, which I would like to briefly outline below.

Humanism

This philosophy is based, first of all, on a fundamental attitude that emphasises the dignity and worth of each individual human being. Secondly, it is based on the belief that people are rational beings who possess within themselves the capacity for truth and goodness. The humanistic concept of the person is based on a model of growth, in which the person is seen as always striving to create, achieve or become. The need for self-fulfilment or self-actualisation is regarded as a fundamental human drive. From a humanistic point of view, fulfilment and growth are achieved through the search for meaning in life and not through supernatural claims. The humanistic view of the person as actively seeking meaning and fulfilment puts a strong focus on the concept of process. Self-actualisation or fulfilment is a continual challenge or journey to be experienced, not an end-state to be attained.

This view of the nature of humanity directly contrasts with the conflict model implicit in psychodynamic theory, and the problem management or coping model implicit in behaviourism. It clearly figures in Rogers' development of the concept of 'A Way of Being' and his notion of 'Becoming a Person', the titles of two of his most well-known books (Rogers, 1961,1980).

Existentialism

Existentialism, broadly defined, is a set of philosophical systems concerned with free will, choice, and personal responsibility. Because we make choices based on our experiences, beliefs, and biases, those choices are unique to us – and made without an objective form of truth. Existentialists believe that there are no 'universal' guidelines for most decisions, no 'rules' by which we all have to live.

Despite encompassing a staggering range of philosophical, religious, and political ideologies, the underlying concepts of existentialism are simple:

- Humankind has free will.
- Life is a series of choices, creating stress.
- Few decisions are without any negative consequences.
- Some things are irrational or absurd, without explanation.
- If one makes a decision, he or she must follow through.
- The only important meaning which can be attached to my life is that which I give to it.

Existentialists conclude that human choice is subjective because individuals finally must make their own choices without help from such external standards as laws, ethical rules, or traditions. Because individuals make their own choices, they are free; but because they freely choose, they are completely responsible for their choices. The existentialists emphasise that freedom is necessarily accompanied by responsibility. Furthermore, since individuals are forced to choose for themselves, they have their freedom – and therefore their responsibility – thrust upon them. In a simple sense we are 'condemned to be free'.

Within existentialism there are several major themes:

1 Concrete individual existence

Existentialists take the view that existence precedes essence for all things. We exist and then we develop a sense of our own essence or nature, from the way we experience ourselves and from the ways in which other people tell us that they experience us.

2 Individual vocation

Existentialists oppose the traditionally held view that there is a common good which is the same for everyone, or a set of rules for living that everyone must abide by. Instead, they insist that the highest good for the individual is to find his or her own unique meaning for their own life, their own unique vocation. Kierkegaard wrote: 'I must find a truth that is true for me ... the idea for which I can live or die' (Dru, [1938] 1967: 15). Other existentialist writers have echoed this belief that one must choose one's own way without the aid of universal, objective standards.

3 Choice and commitment

Perhaps the most prominent theme in existentialism is that of choice and responsibility for the consequences of the choices we make. Most existentialists believe that what differentiates human beings from other creatures is the freedom and the capacity to make choices. Existentialists believe that human beings do not have a fixed nature, or essence, as other animals and plants do. Each human being makes choices that create his or her own nature. Choice is therefore central to human existence, and it is inescapable; even avoidance or the refusal to choose is a choice. That freedom to choose must also be accompanied by commitment to taking the responsibility to live with the consequences of those choices. Existentialists have argued that because individuals are free to choose their own path, they must accept the risk and responsibility of following their commitment wherever it leads.

4 Dread and anxiety

Existentialists believe there are a number of experiences of pain that are common to all human beings. These include the belief that every one experiences a feeling of general apprehension, called 'dread'. (The sense that even on the sunniest day there is a dark cloud on the horizon that will spoil it.) 'Anxiety' is also believed to be a common human experience. This stems from the fact that we can know only three things: we were born, we exist and we will die. Apart from those three, everything else is unknown or conjecture. Anxiety leads to the individual's confrontation with nothingness and with the impossibility of finding ultimate justification for the choices he or she must make. The word 'anguish' is used for the recognition of the total freedom of choice that confronts the individual at every moment and fills them with an unknown and unknowing fear.

Phenomenology

This is a philosophical movement and a method of philosophical inquiry which was developed in the early years of the twentieth century by Edmund Husserl. He identified a set of theoretical approaches that attempt to understand the ways in which people experience the world they create and inhabit. It sets out to study human experience and consciousness in everyday life. The basis of phenomenology is that there is no such thing as a singular reality. There is only the reality that each of us experiences. As a consequence, reality is constructed by each of us and in relational situations can be co-constructed by those in the relationship. A phenomenological approach in therapy is focused on the importance of noticing phenomena occurring. That is, noticing all the events, feelings, experiences, behaviours, words, tones of voice and anything else that we see or hear, as they are in the moment and not interpreting them on the basis of our past experiences. All counsellors, whatever their theoretical approach, need to be phenomenological. We need to notice all the phenomena that are occurring in the client, in ourselves as we work with the client and in the relationship.

In being phenomenological, first, we must try to lay aside all assumptions we have and start afresh. When starting to work with a client, we each time try to imagine that we have never seen this person before, and that we know nothing about them. Contemplate, notice and observe. We need to treat each experience of a client as unique.

Secondly, we must try to achieve an accurate description of what appears to our senses, describing both what we experience and the manner in which we are experiencing it. At the stage of producing verbal descriptions we do not add, subtract, distort, generalise, theorise, explain, or jump to conclusions. We try to avoid the conventional wisdom about the things we observe.

In both existentialism and phenomenology there is an important concept of differentiating between an individual's capacity to be just 'in' their world, like an inanimate object that everything happens to, and 'with' their world, in which the individual really engages and takes responsibility for themselves.

In therapy, in order to discover just how my client is in relation to being 'in' or 'with' their world, I need to really pay attention to the practice of phenomenology and to remember that individuals respond to their world as they uniquely experience it – and not as others see it. Can I really listen to what my client is saying and how they are saying it for clues that will tell me whether they are 'in' or 'with' their world and whether I can work with them in the therapeutic relationship?

To help with being phenomenological, I need to remember that the practice of phenomenology in counselling is systematic and has three rules:

The first is: **The rule of attention**

When encountering anything in ourselves or in our client, we must turn our full attention on to it. Immediately, we are likely to start to try to understand it in terms of past experience. What we need to do instead is just to attend. To see it as if we have never seen it before and to bracket off any assumptions we may make from our own experience of our own world.

On a practice level, we need to be silent. The more we are freed up from having to talk and define or interpret, the more we can listen and be curious about what we consciously notice.

The second is: **The rule of description**

All we have to do is to describe what we *see*, what we experience from the client. We do not have to explain, attribute causation, justify, problem solve, pretend we know more than we do, hypothesise hidden meanings or analyse. On first glance this looks easy. It is not. We are so used to explaining events and fitting them into pre-formed theories in order to make sense of the world that it is very difficult to refrain from doing that.

As a general rule the temptation for the therapist to explain is proportional to their anxiety. Explanation is invariably given to relieve the therapist's own anxiety. If I convince myself I know what is going on, I evade the anxiety of not-knowing. The most useful question to enable a client to understand their experiencing is not: 'Why...?', because that requests a distancing from present experience by attempting to establish mechanistic causal links. However, the question: 'What...?' simply requests further description, as in 'What's that like?', or 'Can you tell me a bit more about that?' Successive re-description will enable us to get nearer to the client's understanding of their experiencing of something than any explanation will. It is also important to remember that existential principle that in life (and in the universe) some things are just absurd and have no explanation.

The third is: **The rule of horizontalisation or equal value**

In applying the rule of horizontalisation we need to consider each part of the content, and of the process, to be of equal importance until we know otherwise. Our ability to horizontalise is related to our ability to identify and deal with our assumptions. Too often we have a tendency to jump to conclusions about our clients on the basis of a superficial match either with our chosen theory or our personal history. We are deciding what is important before the client has told us. We must always be vigilant in trying to avoid this. We must really be engaged not in the search for 'truth' when we are working with a client, but rather in searching for an understanding of the truth as it is for the client. This clearly explains the importance for Rogers of 'checking out' what we sense our client is experiencing, rather than merely reflecting back the words we have heard.

In therapy and in life too, I believe it is important to be phenomenological towards myself as well as towards my client. Can I pay attention to myself at the same time as paying attention to my client? Can I sense how this person and this relationship is impacting on me? What am I feeling? What am I thinking? What am I doing while I am listening to my client? Am I really with my world, here in this moment with my client or am I merely in it? Am I really being authentic and genuine or am I merely playing the role of 'interested' or 'caring' or 'helpful' listener? If I discover that is what I am doing, can I be honest enough with myself to own up to that and stop doing it?

Philosophical principles and basic assumptions

In 1942, Rogers published *Counselling and Psychotherapy*, in which he identified what he saw as the two basic assumptions underpinning the Behaviourist and Psychoanalytic approaches. Namely, that 'the counsellor knows best' and that the job of the counsellor is to lead the client to the goal that the counsellor has chosen.

Rogers then described what he saw as a newer approach to counselling, which had a totally different character from the other approaches and was based on very different beliefs about the nature of human beings. The aim of this new approach was not to solve a particular problem or problems, but to develop a trusting relationship. This relationship would enable the individual to grow, so that they could cope with their current difficulties and with later problems in a more effective manner and thereby become more independent and able to function more effectively.

Rogers argued that human beings are, essentially, positively motivated with a natural internal drive towards growth, health and adjustment. They can be trusted to make choices that enable them to shape, direct and take responsibility for their own existence and the way they live their lives. He believed that human beings need to be enabled to free themselves from internal and external controls imposed by others in order to become fully functioning and to 'heal' themselves. He felt that the natural tendency in any human being was to develop towards becoming a fully functioning individual, with a natural drive to become who we truly are. He developed a strong humanistic belief that the counsellor who enables their client to experience the right growth-promoting conditions in the counselling relationship will enable clients to become more fully functioning; to chose to become their true selves, rather than continuing to be as others want them to be.

For me, that means: Can I focus on really being here with my client, trying to enable them to experience that this bit of their world, with me in it in this room, is a safe enough place for them to be really with me, in our momentarily-shared world? Can I develop a shared understanding with my client of how they experience the phenomenology of their world? Can I work hard to avoid interpreting their experience through the filters of my own experiences and focus on just describing what I experience from and in them? Can I notice all the phenomena that my client brings into the counselling room and treat these as all being of equal value? It seems to me that these humanistic, existential and phenomenological principles are plainly at the root of what Rogers was clearly expressing in the development of the person-centred approach to therapy and to life.

The six necessary and sufficient conditions

In 1957, Rogers published an article that identified the following six fundamental conditions, which he regarded as both necessary and sufficient to establish a counselling relationship, in which therapeutic growth and personality change could occur (Rogers, 1957). These six conditions are:

1 Two persons are in *psychological contact*.
2 The first, whom we shall term the client, is in a state of *incongruence*, being vulnerable or anxious.
3 The second person, whom we shall term the therapist, is *congruent* or *integrated* in the relationship.
4 The therapist experiences *unconditional positive regard* for the client.
5 The therapist experiences an *empathic understanding* of the client's internal frame of reference and endeavours to communicate this experience to the client.
6 The communication to the client of the therapist's empathic understanding and unconditional positive regard is to a minimal degree achieved.

Rogers had an unshakeable belief that if the client can experience these six essential conditions for therapeutic growth, then nothing else is required to enable change to take place in the client. These conditions are both necessary and sufficient in themselves.

All six are the necessary and sufficient conditions

From the very beginning, Rogers referred to all six conditions as 'the necessary and sufficient conditions' for therapeutic growth. However, as the use of the approach developed, three of the conditions (numbers three, four and five), which are perhaps seen to be attributes or attitudes to be integrated in the counsellor, began to receive more prominence and attention than the others. To some extent this still continues today, with these three often being referred to as the 'core conditions'.

This was not a term that Rogers used. I find it intriguing that the term just seemed to appear in the late 1960s. The first mention I have been able to find was the following:

> From an eclectic stance we are free to research the basic core of facilitative conditions, and the selective use of techniques... there is now no need for the artificial dichotomy separating rigor and meaningfulness. ... We have attempted throughout our work to integrate the basic core of facilitative conditions with learning in a social context. (Berenson and Carkhuff, 1967: 448)

Carkhuff was only interested in the three core facilitative conditions and paid no attention to the other three conditions. Rogers himself was strongly convinced that, in therapy, all six conditions were interrelated and of equal importance.

From the late 1960s, perhaps because of Carkhuff's influence, the other three conditions (numbers one, two and six) seem to have been given less attention, perhaps because they are rather more like aspects of the relationship between counsellor and client. Rogers himself believed that condition one, psychological contact, was an absolute prerequisite for therapy to take place. For me, of equal importance was Rogers' hypothesis that the communication to the client of conditions four (unconditional positive regard) and five (empathic understanding) is achieved to at least a minimal degree.

For the counsellors who want to commit themselves to the person-centred approach, it is important to remember that all six conditions are of equal importance. They are rather like the pieces in a jigsaw – they all need to be present in some way in the counselling relationship in order to see the full picture. This does not mean that they all have to be present to the same degree all the time. That would probably be impossible to achieve, even for Carl Rogers. It does mean that all six need to be present in some way and the communication of the three central conditions needs to be experienced by the client to at least a minimal degree during counselling.

The interrelationship between the six conditions

Retaining Rogers' concept that all six conditions are necessary and sufficient, in order to help explore and explain them I will refer to conditions three, four and five as the 'central conditions', and conditions one, two and six as the 'further conditions'.

Because of the prominence that has been given to the three central conditions, anyone setting out to practise as a person-centred counsellor may find it difficult to understand the equal importance of all six conditions, the interrelationship between them and, in particular, the pivotal role of the first condition, around which the other five conditions seem to revolve. It can be said that in the counselling relationship the other five conditions are meaningless without the presence of the first condition. This is because the first condition, psychological contact, is about counsellor and client having a real relationship, rather than two people just being in a room together. It is also very clear that relationships do not just happen without any effort. Even in everyday life, we usually have to want a relationship to happen and to do something about making it happen and to work at maintaining it. This is no less true of the counselling relationship and of establishing psychological contact between counsellor and client.

It is also very clear that the sixth condition (the communication to the client of the therapist's empathic understanding and unconditional positive regard is to a minimal degree achieved) is essential. Counselling can hardly be effective if the client doesn't actually experience the counsellor as being empathic or having unconditional positive regard for them.

Necessary and sufficient

Today, there is a growing and more general acceptance that the central conditions are important for any therapist, whatever approach they use, although other approaches do not accept that these conditions are sufficient in themselves to enable change to take place.

For Rogers, however, these conditions were more than just essential. He believed that they were entirely sufficient, on their own, to enable therapeutic growth to be possible. He argued strongly that the experiencing of those three central conditions by the client, in the therapist, creates a strongly therapeutic relationship and therefore there was no need for techniques of any sort. He also firmly believed that these conditions could not be 'turned on' in counselling as a kind of technique. Instead, they needed to be developed as an integrated part of the counsellor's personality, and to be rooted in the counsellor having those fundamental beliefs about human nature which are described above, along with the counsellor's belief in the client's capacity to achieve their own potential to become fully functioning.

The stages of becoming fully functioning in counselling

Rogers held the belief that the ideal state for any human being is to be in a state of becoming, to be always striving to become a fully functioning person. Through his interest in research into the outcomes of counselling, he developed a belief that it was important to develop some understanding of the way in which change takes place in individuals through counselling. In particular, he wanted to find a way to describe the process which takes place in the counselling relationship. Through further research into his own practice, he developed his theory of the seven stages of process (Rogers, 1961: 125–59). He saw these stages as a flowing continuum rather than seven fixed and discrete stages. It is important to emphasise that this is not a rigid model, but is offered to explain the kind of processes that a client might experience. A brief outline of these stages is as follows:

Stage One: The client is very defensive and extremely resistant to change.

Stage Two: The client becomes slightly less rigid and will talk about external events or other people.

Stage Three: The client talks about him/herself, but as an object and avoids discussion of present events.

Stage Four: The client begins to talk about deep feelings and develops a relationship with the counsellor.

Stage Five: The client can express present emotions and is beginning to rely more on his/her own decision-making abilities and increasingly accepts more responsibility for his/her actions.

Stage Six: The client shows rapid growth towards congruence and begins to develop unconditional positive regard for others. This stage signals the end of the need for formal therapy.

Stage Seven: The client is a fully functioning, self-actualising individual who is empathic and shows unconditional positive regard for others. This individual can relate their previous therapy to present-day real-life situations.

It is also important to remember that the client will flow backwards and forwards along that continuum and will not automatically progress along it as though they are discreet steps.

Rogers wrote eloquently about what he perceived as these seven stages that an individual passes through in therapy in the journey towards becoming. I will explore them in more depth in Chapter 5.

Self-actualisation

In developing his theories, Rogers was profoundly influenced by the writings of a number of other psychologists and philosophers. In particular, he was strongly influenced by the thinking of Kurt Goldstein, a Jewish-German psychiatrist who first developed the term 'self-actualisation' (Goldstein, 1939). This was a term that Rogers also used, although rather more broadly than Goldstein had defined it. Rogers referred instead to the 'actualising tendency', which he believed was the principal basic tendency in all human beings, the tendency to want to become the self that one truly is, rather than the self that others want us to be.

Goldstein also influenced Abraham Maslow, another psychologist whose thinking Rogers also drew upon, and who was developing his own theories of personality development. Maslow's most famous concept was that of a hierarchy of needs (Maslow, 1943). The inner core of human nature, argued Maslow, consists of urges and instinctive tendencies that create basic needs within the person. These needs have to be satisfied, otherwise frustration and sickness will result. The first and most basic needs are physiological and are related to survival. These include the need for food and shelter. If these physiological needs are not satisfied, all other needs are temporarily pushed aside. Once basic physiological needs are fulfilled, relatively higher needs emerge, such as those for safety, love and esteem. When safety needs are satisfied, love and esteem needs arise and the individual will focus on meeting these needs.

The self-actualising tendency and the fully functioning person

At the top of the hierarchy of needs, Maslow placed the need for self-actualisation, which arose from the emergence of a need to know, a need to satisfy our curiosity about nature, a need to understand the perplexities of life and ourselves. Maslow and Rogers both drew close parallels between Maslow's self-actualising person, whose most basic drive was the desire to become all that one is capable of becoming, and Rogers' fully functioning person, whose basic drive was to become the person that one truly is. Rogers believed that the actualising tendency could be inhibited but could never be destroyed, except by death, and that it was directed only towards positive objectives, to enable the individual to function to the best of their ability in whatever conditions they might find themselves. Another significant difference between Maslow and Rogers was that Maslow believed that self-actualisation was a state that could actually be achieved, while Rogers believed that self-actualisation was a process with a continuing potential for further growth.

Rogers' theory of personality and behaviour

The Policy and Planning Board of the American Psychological Association invited a number of leaders in the fields of psychology and psychotherapy to contribute to a seven-volume series entitled *Psychology: A Study of a Science* (Koch (ed.), 1959). Carl Rogers, along with the other contributors to the first three volumes, was assigned the task of describing his current theoretical formulations, which he considered to be of recent importance to psychology. His chapter was entitled 'A theory of therapy, personality and interpersonal relationships as developed in the client-centered framework'. This was later reproduced as Chapter 11 in *Client Centred Therapy* (Rogers, 1979).

Rogers describes 19 propositions, giving his theoretical view of the nature of human personality and how it works. These propositions are written in the rather technical language of an academic writing for other academics. Although this makes them a little difficult to read, trying to translate them into more readable everyday language seems to rob them of their true meaning in the context of the time that they were written and their purpose. I will therefore present them as they were written.

I   Every individual exists in a continually changing world of experience of which he is the centre.

II The organism reacts to the field as it is experienced and perceived. This perceptual field is, for the individual, 'reality'.

III The organism reacts as an organized whole to this phenomenal field.

IV The organism has one basic tendency and striving – to actualize, maintain, and enhance the experiencing organism.

V   Behavior is basically the goal-directed attempt of the organism to satisfy its needs as experienced, in the field as perceived.

VI Emotion accompanies and in general facilitates such goal-directed behavior, the kind of emotion being related to the seeking versus the consummatory aspects of the behavior, and the intensity of the emotion being related to the perceived significance of the behavior for the maintenance and enhancement of the organism.

VII The best vantage point for understanding behavior is from the internal frame of reference of the individual himself.

VIII A portion of the total perceptual field gradually becomes differentiated as the self.

IX As a result of interaction with the environment, and particularly as a result of evaluational interaction with others, the structure of self is formed – an organized, fluid, but consistent conceptual pattern of perceptions of characteristics and relationships of the 'I' or the 'me', together with values attached to these concepts.

X   The values attached to experiences, and the values which are a part of the self structure, in some instances are values experienced directly by the organism, and in some instances are values introjected or taken over from others, but perceived in distorted fashion, as if they had been experienced directly.

XI As experiences occur in the life of the individual, they are either (a) symbolized, perceived, and organized into some relationship to the self, (b) ignored because there is no perceived relationship to the self structure, (c) denied symbolization or given a distorted symbolization because the experience is inconsistent with the structure of the self.

XII   Most of the ways of behaving which are adopted by the organism are those which are consistent with the concept of self.

XIII   Behavior may, in some instances, be brought about by organic experiences and needs which have not been symbolized. Such behavior may be inconsistent with the structure of the self, but in such instances the behavior is not 'owned' by the individual.

XIV   Psychological maladjustment exists when the organism denies to awareness significant sensory and visceral experiences, which consequently are not symbolized and organized into the gestalt of the self-structure. When this situation exists, there is a basic or potential psychological tension.

XV   Psychological adjustment exists when the concept of the self is such that all the sensory and visceral experiences of the organism are, or may be, assimilated on a symbolic level into a consistent relationship with the concept of self.

XVI   Any experience which is inconsistent with the organization or structure of self may be perceived as a threat, and the more of these perceptions there are, the more rigidly the self-structure is organized to maintain itself.

XVII   Under certain conditions, involving primarily complete absence of any threat to the self-structure, experiences which are inconsistent with it may be perceived, and examined, and the structure of self revised to assimilate and include such experiences.

XVIII When the individual perceives and accepts into one consistent and integrated system all his sensory and visceral experiences, then he is necessarily more understanding of others and is more accepting of others as separate individuals.

XIX   As the individual perceives and accepts into his self-structure more of his organic experiences, he finds that he is replacing his present value *system* based so largely upon introjections which have been distortedly symbolized with a continuing organismic valuing process. (Rogers, 1959: 184–256)

Referring back to the section on philosophy above, there are many points within the 19 propositions where clear connections can be made with humanistic, existential and phenomenological principles and explain various aspects of the person-centred approach. Perhaps one of the most important of these propositions is the one which states that the 'organism reacts as an organized whole to its experiencing of its phenomenological field' (Rogers, 1951: 484). This is broadly taken to mean that no one part of the personality acts entirely on its own behalf, but that parts of the self which are fragile or vulnerable and may perhaps have been damaged, will be helped, supported and even protected by other parts of the personality as they respond to their experience of life. This has led to an important aspect of the person-centred approach, which is that of attending to the 'whole' person, with the whole of the self of the therapist. This means that as counsellors we need to be accepting, empathic and genuinely present both with and for all aspects of the client's personality and not just those parts that we like or are drawn to, and to be present with the whole of ourselves. To illustrate, I will briefly describe some of my work with a client for whom it was really important that I was completely accepting of her whole person, including the part of her that wanted to deny the pain that she was experiencing.

The communication and experiencing of unconditional acceptance

I recall Patricia, a middle-aged, female client who presented with a very bubbly, cheerful personality, always smiling and talking in a positive way. She had been referred to me because she was having difficulties in all of the important relationships in her life. She seemed to have no capacity at all to express feelings of anger, frustration, disappointment, sadness, loss or fear. She seemed to continually try to convince herself that everything would be alright providing she put on a brave face and remained cheerful.

I noticed how when she talked about some of her disappointments and difficulties, she would slump down in her chair with quite a sad expression on her face and that tears would come to her eyes, which she would rapidly wipe away. She would then, literally, give herself a shake, sit upright, grit her teeth and smile before making one of her 'Well – it will all be alright if I stay positive, won't it?' statements.

I said that I had noticed this happening several times and how puzzled I was by this behaviour. I wondered what it would be like for her to stay with her feelings of sadness or disappointment. 'I can't do that' she said strongly. 'Ever since I was a little girl I've been taught to put a brave face on things and that if I do, they will get better.' She paused for a moment or two and then added in a very quiet and reflective voice, 'But I guess they don't always do that, do they?'

I responded with 'Well, Patricia, I'm not saying you shouldn't do what you have been taught to do, even if you know it doesn't always work. I guess there are times when it has been really useful. What I am saying is that here, in this room, it is OK for you to choose to be with these uncomfortable feelings, because it is safe enough to do that. I feel that it would be OK for you to experience and talk here with me about all that disappointment and sadness that you have. I won't think any worse of you if you do. In fact, I'll be really pleased if you can share those feelings with me. I'd feel privileged by that rather than feeling you are shutting me out.'

After some quiet thought, she replied, 'Do you mean it is alright for me to have these feelings, you're saying that I am allowed to have them?'

'Dead right,' I said. 'If I was experiencing some of the difficulties you are describing, I think I would feel pretty sad and disappointed too. Those feelings may not be comfortable or nice, but they are your feelings and I think it is pretty important to value and take care of them, rather than pretending that they don't exist. It's a bit like saying to yourself that your pain doesn't matter – and I think that it does matter to you a great deal.'

'I'll have to think about that,' she said. 'Don't know if I can do it, though.'

'That's OK.' I said. 'No hurry. I'd just like to be able to get a real sense of how it feels to be Patricia, living with all that pain and never able to share it with anyone.'

In experiencing my acceptance of all the parts of her personality, she eventually began to be able to be more accepting of that part of her which was in so much pain and much more able to choose not to defend it by pretending it did not exist.

Phenomenological observation

This extract also demonstrates another important principle in the person-centred approach which we perhaps use in a different way from the other approaches. The technical term for this is phenomenology, the observation of phenomena – things that happen. That is, the importance of careful observation of everything the client does and says in the relationship and the communication of how the counsellor experiences all these aspects of the client, in a non-judgemental way. Above, I show how I noticed the apparent conflict between the feelings Patricia was describing and how she was behaving. I fed this back in an accepting, non-judgemental manner, without interpreting it in any way. I sought to find out what this behaviour meant to her, so that both she and I could begin to understand. This, I think, gave her an opportunity to think about what she was doing and the consequences of behaving in that way. Through that, Patricia began to recognise that she could choose to behave differently, rather than continue to do as her parents had taught her and that there would be quite different and more positive consequences arising from her changed behaviour.

The avoidance of technique and developing a way of being

I referred earlier to Rogers' view that the six conditions could not and should not be used as a kind of technique but that they need to be developed from within a deeply held belief in the positive nature of human beings and their actualising tendency, as an integrated part of the counsellor's personality. If this happens in counselling, the client will experience those conditions in abundance in the relationship. In this process, Rogers believed that the client, in experiencing these conditions in the counsellor, will experience themselves as being fully, psychologically 'received' by the counsellor (Rogers, 1961). Any attempt to use those conditions as a technique, without those strongly held beliefs, will be experienced by the client as false and lacking in genuineness and is unlikely to provide the relationship or the therapeutic climate in which change can occur.

Rogers took this further to develop the most significant difference between the person-centred approach to counselling and other approaches. This lies in the belief that the experiencing of the three central conditions is important in every relationship and in every aspect of life. The person-centred approach has become more than a way of developing a therapeutic relationship with clients. Rogers described it as 'a life-affirming way of being' (Rogers, 1980). This has led to the person-centred approach being described as a quiet revolution.

A link to the next chapter

In the next chapter, I will explore two fundamental beliefs held by Carl Rogers, his understanding of the characteristics of the actualising tendency and of the fully functioning person. I will also look at Rogers' belief in trusting that the client is the only expert in their own internal world and the importance of avoiding being an expert and doing the utmost to have a non-directive attitude.

Recommended reading

Macmillan, Michael (2004) *The Person-centred Approach to Therapeutic Change.* Sage Therapeutic Change Series. London: Sage.

Rogers, Carl R. (1990) 'The necessary and sufficient conditions for therapeutic personality change', in Howard Kirshenbaum and Valerie Land Henderson (eds), *The Carl Rogers Reader.* London: Constable, Chapter 16.

Thorne, Brian (2003) *Carl Rogers*. Key Figures in Counselling and Psychotherapy Series. London: Sage.

Wilkins, Paul (2010) *Person-centred Therapy – 100 Key points*. London and New York: Routledge.

Worsley, R. (2002) *Process Work in Person-centred Therapy: Phenomenological and Existential Perspectives*. Ross-on-Wye: PCCS Books.

TWO

The Beliefs Underpinning the Person-Centred Approach

In this chapter, I will begin by looking at the basic beliefs held by Rogers about the nature of the universe and of humanity. These helped Rogers to identify the nature and characteristics of the self-actualising process and led to the development of his notion of the fully functioning person and the development of the person-centred approach. I will look briefly at Rogers' belief in the importance of fully accepting the client's experiencing of their reality. Then I will touch on the importance of holding a non-directive attitude and the interrelationship between the six necessary and sufficient conditions for therapeutic growth. I will also briefly consider the issue of what I call '*therapeutic intent*' and the validity of the person-centred approach in short-term therapy.

The two basic assumptions

In order to better understand Rogers' ideas about the necessary and sufficient conditions for therapeutic growth, anyone aspiring to be a person-centred counsellor needs to have a clear understanding and a general acceptance of Rogers' two fundamental beliefs that he held about the nature of the universe and the nature of human beings. It was out of these beliefs that Rogers developed his theory of personality and behaviour and the concept of the six necessary and sufficient conditions for therapeutic growth. He saw these two beliefs as the basic foundation stones of the person-centred approach. These two beliefs or assumptions that Rogers held, which I shall now describe, are 'the formative tendency' and the 'actualising tendency'.

The formative tendency

Up until the time that Rogers began to develop his theories, scientists had generally taken a rather gloomy view of life and had paid far more attention to the universal processes of death and deterioration or disorder – a process known as entropy. A great deal was known about the ways in which planetary systems, organisations and physical organisms, such as plants and human beings, had a tendency to deteriorate and die. As a result of his own experiencing of life, his own scientific studies and his reading of the work of other scientists, Rogers began to challenge this sole focus on a negative process. He took the view that there was an equal if not more important process in existence, which was being ignored. He suggested that attention should be turned to a more important formative tendency in which the universe could be seen to be constantly expanding and that everything in the universe followed that tendency, to develop and become more complex (Rogers, 1980). This matches a well-known law of physics, that for every force there is an equal and opposite force. It makes sense, then, that the natural tendency towards entropy in us should be opposed by a natural tendency to grow and develop. I am somewhat surprised that, in his later writing, Rogers ignored the tendency towards entropy and focused on the actualising tendency as the one fundamental tendency in human beings. For myself, I believe in the law of physics, that for every force there is an equal and opposite force. As a consequence, I believe that entropy must always be at work in opposition to the formative tendency or perhaps that the formative tendency is always at work in opposition to and will overcome entropy, if those necessary and sufficient conditions are present.

A universal tendency

Rogers suggested that this formative tendency could be observed at every level of existence in the universe. The most straightforward evidence of this, for him, was in the observable fact that the joining together of two single cells through fertilisation begins a process of continuous development and growth leading to the birth of the highly complex human infant. He believed it was important not to ignore the tendency towards deterioration but, more importantly, to give full attention to the universal formative process. His fundamental belief was that while the universe and everything within it is deteriorating, more importantly, it is also always in the process of building and creating, growing and developing, becoming more and more complicated. In addition to Rogers' belief, I see that process of deterioration and death as an important step towards the next stage of birth and further growth, as part of a continuing cycle of growth and decay. I know that for myself and for many of my clients, that we have needed to get worse before we could begin to get better. Often getting worse or deteriorating is an important stage in the process of self-actualisation. Through the process of enabling a client to experience and explore their deepest, most painful emotions, they can indeed feel that they are getting worse or deteriorating. The experiencing of those feelings within the necessary and sufficient conditions in a safe, containing relationship with the counsellor, will enable the formative tendency to take precedence and for the client to become more fully functioning.

The value of deterioration

An example of the value of deterioration as a step towards self-actualisation occurred when I worked with a client some years ago. Jean came to see me originally with symptoms of depression and anxiety with which she seemed to be really battling. She clearly held a strong view that she should not be depressed, that it was not acceptable to be unhappy and that she must do everything she could to be happy and positive. She must not allow herself to worry about all the things that were wrong in her life and she had come to see me to help her to get rid of her depression.

Over the next three months, I experienced Jean working hard to deny all her bad feelings and forcing herself to 'get better', as she put it.

She identified different ways of dealing with the symptoms, reducing the feelings of sadness and the anxiety attacks and doing her utmost to avoid staying with the feelings of unhappiness and anger at the various situations in her life.

Feeling better, she decided she did not need to see me any more and off she went. I accepted that she felt better and wished her well, though I wondered to myself how long it would be before I would see her again, as I was sure that she had just put metaphorical sticking plasters on her wounds and that those wounds would flare up again. Of course, I did not mention this to her, believing in the importance of trusting in her knowing what was best for herself at that time.

Sure enough in three months' time she came back to see me but seemed even more depressed. We repeated the counselling process in almost exactly the same way and again, after a few months, she left apparently feeling better. Four months after that she came back again even more depressed and anxious and clearly very frightened that she was never going to be able to completely recover.

This time, while I was very accepting of her belief that she needed to force herself to get better, I wondered out loud to her what it might be like if she stopped trying to force herself to get better and allowed herself to really experience all the sad, unhappy feelings that she was trying to repress. I said to her, 'It seems to me like the more you try to force these feelings to go away, the more they fight back.'

Jean paused for a moment and then replied, 'Yes, it does sound like they want to be heard, doesn't it?'

I continued, 'I know these feelings are very unpleasant for you and you feel you shouldn't have them. I also get a sense that you are very frightened of these feelings and somehow that if you let them out they will take control and might even destroy you. I know they are very unpleasant for you – but for me, there is nothing wrong with having those feelings. I wonder what would happen if you were to really allow them to be present, perhaps even to take care of them rather than trying to destroy them?'

After a long pause, Jean said, 'Well it does feel like the more I try to fight these feelings, even though I get a bit better for a while, I just end up getting worse and worse. Perhaps I just need to take the risk of letting go and being really depressed?'

I nodded acceptingly and said, 'I can hear in your voice just how scary that is and the fear that if you go all the way down you may never come up again.'

After a pause she said, 'Well I don't think I can do it on my own. I'm going to need some help. Will you help me with that?'

Over the next two years I worked with Jean as she allowed herself to sink fully into experiencing all her feelings of depression and through this she was able to get in touch with feelings she was not aware she had. She found the feelings of anger, frustration, rejection, disappointment and desperation that her feelings of depression had prevented her from experiencing. Through allowing herself to, as she saw it, sink into experiencing these feelings of depression, she began to lose her fear of them as she discovered that they did not actually annihilate her. This enabled her to become aware of and to get in touch with other strong feelings where she had previously denied their existence. Over time, she began to value all these feelings and to be able to use them productively. It took a long time but eventually she began to emerge as a new and very different person, able to function more fully and with much greater autonomy.

The actualising tendency

Rogers' belief in that fundamental formative tendency of the universe and everything within it led him to his second fundamental belief, that there is a positive, formative, developmental tendency inherent in all organisms, including human beings. He took the view that the basic driving force in all human beings is a positive drive to achieve their potential, to self-actualise and to become a fully functioning person. He believed also that this actualising tendency should be trusted and that even in the worst conditions human beings will strive to be as healthy and successful as they can be – that human beings will always move towards growth and towards becoming fully functioning. He believed that the self-actualising drive is the one central source of energy for human beings, perhaps even present in our DNA.

Rogers recognised that this actualising tendency could become thwarted or twisted by experiences but that only death could actually destroy it. He accepted that there is an opposite tendency in the universe, which is towards deterioration and death, and this tendency is also present in human beings. He saw these two tendencies as existing side by side but that while accepting the presence of a tendency for deterioration and death, this needed to be seen within the overall human tendency to grow and develop. In the individual given poor or negative conditions and treatment, the tendency to deteriorate and not to grow might take over. However, he felt that given the right, positive conditions, the actualising tendency was bound to succeed, because it is the fundamental drive in all of us. Importantly, he saw that actualising tendency as a drive to become more fully functioning.

In Jean, I experienced someone who allowed herself to experience the disintegrative tendency towards deterioration in herself. Then, through experiencing those necessary and sufficient conditions in counselling, she began to discover her self-actualising tendency, becoming able to function more fully in her world, rather than being ruled by her past experiences.

Towards the end of our work together, she made an interesting observation. She said, 'Although in some ways I am much happier, life seems very much harder for me now. Before, I just used to fight against my feelings all the time. These days, I face up to them and don't pretend that they are not there, or try and make light of what is happening to me. It does mean that life does feel tougher when I have to really face up to things and deal with them.'

I said, 'That sounds as though you might be a bit angry with me for enabling you to get to become that way?'

'Oh, I am,' she said. 'And I'm also grateful that you challenged me to do it and seemed to really believe that I could. I don't want to go back to how I was before. This is tough at times and I know that it is actually much better, because at last I am in charge of me!'

For me, I experienced a new Jean, able to function more fully as a human being, with some real autonomy. She seemed more able to live in the moment with all her feelings and to face up to life, and I and she both knew she would live it more resourcefully after counselling had finished.

Characteristics of the actualising tendency

To gain a better understanding of self-actualisation, let us consider a number of characteristics of the process, which have been identified.

The unique and universal tendency

While Rogers described self-actualisation as a universal tendency in human beings, at the same time he held a strong belief that each person is unique and individual. Therefore, it is important to remember that the way in which the self-actualising tendency is shown will be uniquely different in every individual. There is no single way of self-actualising that will fit every human being. It is also true that the ways in which we self-actualise will vary for each of us at different times and in different contexts. Self-actualisation is a process which is both universal, in that it is a tendency in all of us, and at the same time it is also unique and individual, in the ways in which it will be achieved and expressed.

The ever-present tendency

Rogers believed firmly that the actualising process is always present in each of us, continually seeking to enable to maintain and enhance ourselves and our experience of life. He accepted that the tendency could be diverted or warped by situations or the difficult or unpleasant experiences we might have, but that even in the worst of conditions we seek to do the best for ourselves. He also believed that the actualising tendency could only be completely thwarted by death (Rogers, 1980). It is also true that self-actualisation is not always about doing what is good or right or appropriate. Sometimes we can only develop and grow through doing things that are wrong or inappropriate, testing out what works for us and developing through that. Sometimes it is only by making mistakes and getting things wrong that we can learn from them.

Increased autonomy

An important aspect of the actualising tendency is that it is best experienced in the growing autonomy of the individual and a decreased tendency to be dependent on other people for approval or direction. The self-actualising person is one who is moving away from always behaving or doing as their parents or significant others taught them they should, to a situation where they choose more often to behave or to do what they themselves believe is right for them. While not totally ignoring the impact of their actions on other people, they are able to choose to do or say something and not be prevented from that because they think it might upset someone else. The self-actualising person is more aware of the choices that they have and has a greater capacity to make those choices for themselves and to live with the consequences.

Increased consciousness and self-awareness

Another important characteristic of the actualising tendency is that it only becomes effective as the individual becomes more self-aware and more open to their experiencing of themselves and their life. Through becoming more self-aware and through being more open to our experiences, we become more aware that we have choices and the capacity to make them. The more an individual is able to be open and to accept the feelings they are experiencing, the more they will be able to be as they are feeling, to be real, to be authentic and to be independent of others' control. It is important to believe that there is no feeling we should not have and to be able to be aware of and to acknowledge and own the feelings we experience, and to value them all equally. This seemed such an important element of Jean's growth. The more she experienced my acceptance of her with all her feelings, the more she became able to accept herself and her feelings, and to be able to choose to be different.

Living fully in the moment

Rogers also believed that an important aspect of the self-actualising process was the capacity to live fully in the moment, as things happen or are experienced, rather than to be continually preoccupied with what has happened in the past or what might happen in the future. This means developing the capacity to be accepting of life as something which is fluid and always changing, something that we can choose how we react to. This means we need to recognise that although there may be similarities in experiences we have had before, they are never exactly the same and neither are we exactly the same in any situation. It is important that we allow ourselves to experience what is happening now and allow ourselves to respond fluidly to that, rather than forcing ourselves to react as we always have, to what seem to be similar experiences in the past.

Trust in the self

The process of self-actualisation is clearly enhanced as we develop and strengthens our capacity to trust in ourselves and our reactions to new situations, rather than being told what to do, think or feel by other people or by sets of rules created by other people or institutions. The more self-aware we become, the more we are open to our experiencing, the more we will be able to trust our own internal reactions to our experiencing of people, events and situations and the more we will be able to do what feels right to us and feel OK with that. This will, of course, allow us to be more able to make mistakes and to learn from them, which will further enhance our capacity to trust in ourselves and our judgements. Trust in the self will also encompass the developing ability to own and value our feelings and to reserve the right to express our feelings because it feels right to do so. None of our feelings is intrinsically 'bad'. They may be uncomfortable, unpleasant or painful and, similarly, some of our feelings may be pleasant and enjoyable, but none of them is intrinsically 'good'. All our feelings need to be owned and valued equally in order to understand them.

The fully functioning person

These characteristics of the self-actualising process enable us as individuals to move towards becoming more fully functioning and enable us to be more psychologically free. In summary, what Rogers was saying is that the more fully functioning person is able to:

- be more in touch with and to live with all of his/her feelings and reactions,
- make use of all the information that comes to him/her through being open to all of their experiencing,
- live in the moment rather than being trapped in the past or the future,
- function more freely in making choices that are truly theirs,
- experience all of his/her feelings and to be less afraid of any of them,
- be more open to the consequences of his/her actions and to be more accepting and able to correct them when they go wrong,
- be completely engaged in the process of being and becoming, in a more fluid and open way.

The changing world of experience

Rogers suggested that each of us is at the centre of a continually changing world of experience and that we are only consciously aware of some aspects of that experience (Rogers, 1951). What is important about this idea is Rogers' suggestion that the only person who can truly understand an individual's experiencing of their world is that individual themselves. The world of our experiences, feelings and sensations is, for each of us, a very private world which only we can understand. Here, then, is the basis of the identification of the need for unconditional acceptance as one of the six necessary and sufficient conditions for therapeutic growth.

Acceptance as the basis for trust, that the client is the only expert in their own internal world

Rogers is often quoted as saying that the counsellor must always trust in the wisdom of the client. What he said more often, and what he meant when he used that phrase, is that it is important for the counsellor to always remember *that the client is the only expert in their own internal world.* The client is the only one who really knows what it feels like to be them and the only one who really knows how they experience their world, their feelings and their reality. For Rogers, this level of full and unconditional acceptance of the client's experiencing of themselves and their reality was essential to create trust in the relationship. I will build on the example I gave of Margaret in Chapter 1, by offering another example from my practice in order to emphasise further and to deliberately restate the importance of this concept, in my work as a counsellor.

A young man, Steve, came to see me at the suggestion of his GP. He arrived looking very agitated, sweating quite profusely and with large dark red blotches on his face and neck. After the usual beginning process of setting the agreement for how we might work together, he began to tell me his concerns.

He was in his late twenties and lived at home with his father, who had been separated from Steve's mother for some years. He was a little above average height, similar in height and build to me, in fact. He looked quite fit, with short hair and a not unpleasant face and was dressed quite smartly, looking quite presentable. Steve said that he worked in an engineering company as an administrative assistant and enjoyed his work. He told me that his problem was that he was really anxious about meeting new people and that he found it really difficult to make friends. He spent a lot of time on his own and did not go out very often, saying he preferred to read or watch TV. The reason for this was that he had these attacks of blushing and fierce sweating and he believed that anyone who saw this would know that there was something wrong with him.

I responded by saying, tentatively, 'So, you feel really nervous when you are going to meet new people? You're scared stiff that you are just going to blush scarlet and sweat streams when you meet them? You believe that if they see you doing that they will think you are strange in some way and you will be really embarrassed?'

Steve nodded in reply, looking at me rather suspiciously.

I continued, 'So is that what you think I might be doing now? That I must be thinking there is something wrong with you because your face and neck are red and you're sweating quite a bit?'

He sat there, continuing to nod in agreement as I said, 'Well, I can understand you worrying about what I might think, particularly as we don't know each other. I have noticed that you are a bit red and sweating a bit, but that hasn't made me think there is anything wrong with you. What I do wonder is if *you* think there is something wrong with you? And perhaps it might be helpful for you to know that I am actually feeling a bit nervous at meeting you for the first time because I always feel nervous at meeting new people!'

After a silence, he looked down at his feet and said, 'Well, I know there is something wrong with me. I'm weird! I keep getting all these red blotches when I might be going to meet someone new. I know I look weird to other people.'

My immediate internal reaction was that I wanted to tell him that was nonsense, that he didn't look weird to me at all. Instead I responded quite tentatively with, 'You sound like you feel really fed up with looking like you do and that when you meet people they are bound to think you are very strange? It also sounds like you really believe that you look odd, especially when you get these red blotches on your face? It also sounds as though you feel you are not in control of yourself and that is really quite scary?'

For the rest of that session I concentrated on really trying to hear how Steve felt about himself and how other people might perceive him. Much as I wanted to, I did not try to tell him that he wasn't strange or unusual looking or deformed in any way. He did not look like that to me but it was really important that he experienced my acceptance of his feelings and perceptions, from his view point. How Steve felt about himself was clearly having a huge impact on the way he was living his life. He was becoming increasingly distressed by it and increasingly dysfunctional, hiding himself away from other people more and more as time passed.

This accepting response to Steve and to his experiencing of his reality enabled him to begin a fairly lengthy counselling relationship with me. Through this relationship he began to find different ways of reacting to how he experienced himself, which eventually led to him being much more accepting of himself and learning to function in a much more effective way. At the end of our relationship, Steve said that probably the most important thing for him had been that I had not told him that he should not feel that way and that I had not asked him why he felt like that.

To refer back to the often-quoted phrase, 'trusting in the wisdom of the client', Rogers was definitely not saying that the client always knows best. Clearly there are many times that clients do not know best what choices to make or how to be. Neither was Rogers denying the wisdom of the counsellor. What he was stating very firmly was that each of us is the only expert in our own internal worlds of feeling and experiencing. The job of the counsellor is to work hard at getting a clear and unambiguous understanding of how each client experiences their internal world and to communicate understanding and acceptance of that to the client. So many times I have realised that the experiencing of this in the counselling relationship has enabled clients to begin to be accepting of their experiencing and to begin to be more accepting of themselves and more able to change and grow.

The question 'why?' can only be answered by the client

The example of Steve also illustrates another of Rogers' propositions, that the best place to understand someone's behaviour is through how that person experiences their behaviour (Rogers, 1951). The individual is the only one who is likely to understand or know why they behave or react in the way that they do, as a consequence of their experiencing of their world and all that they experience within it. For that reason, when clients ask (as they so often do) 'Why do I do this?', 'Why do I feel like this?', 'Why is this happening?', I have to say as gently and as firmly as possible, 'I don't know. In fact I can't know. All I do know is that this is how you really feel and it seems very uncomfortable for you. You are the only one who has any possibility of answering that question.' As a person-centred counsellor, I cannot give them the answers they are looking for. I can only be very accepting of their fears and concerns and try to help them to find those answers for themselves, if they exist. This can be very frustrating for both the client and the counsellor. After all, we live in a world which is always seeking solutions and answers and it can be very hard to accept that for some problems there are no solutions and for some questions there are no answers. An existentialist perspective is that some things in life are just absurd, incapable of explanation, they just 'are'. It is important that I communicate my understanding of a client's strong desire to know 'why' and their anxiety and frustration at not being able to answer the question. I also need to make sure that I do not take those feelings into myself and start to try to provide answers for a client, but hopefully I will strive to enable them to discover and come to terms with the notion that the issue they are struggling with is a 'fact of life'. It just *is* that way and is not open to being changed.

Directive versus non-directive

This links very much to another contentious and often misunderstood aspect of the person-centred approach. Originally, Rogers described the approach as 'non-directive' (Rogers, 1942), which has led to some misunderstandings. Rogers, in describing 'non-directive therapy', focused on the counsellor depending on the client's own internal resources and the client's capacity to solve their own problems, with the counsellor acting as a facilitator to this process. Rogers recognised that complete non-directivity was an ideal that was impossible to achieve. What he believed was important was that the counsellor had a non-directive attitude or stance, really holding on to the belief that they were not there to direct the client or tell the client what to do. My view is that, as a counsellor, I am there to help the client to identify what choices are open to them and to decide for themselves, without influence by me, which choices they want to take, including deciding not to choose. Clearly there are times when the client's safety or the safety of others is at risk, that the counsellor may have an ethical responsibility to intervene. It is impossible to be completely non-directive. The choices that I make in response to my client, in relation to what feelings I choose to check out, whether I choose to remain silent or to speak, the words that I choose to use in responding may often be experienced by the client as directive, no matter how much I intend them not to be. I guess many counsellors will have experienced working in a very empathic and accepting way with a client, doing their utmost not to be directive or tell the client what they should or shouldn't do. Then in the next session, the client comes in and says 'Well, I did what you told me to…'. It may well be that in some unconscious way I have actually inferred some direction I think the client should go in. It may also be that I actually was very non-directive and yet directiveness was just what the client experienced.

The integrated relationship between the necessary and sufficient conditions

Throughout Rogers' description of his theory of personality and behaviour there is a very clear suggestion that through the experiencing of the six conditions in counselling, an individual can develop the capacity to become more accepting of themselves and their experiencing of their feelings. In doing this, they will begin to develop their own system of values, will be more able to judge themselves and will become less dependent on other people's judgements about them. Through the process of becoming more self-aware and more understanding of themselves, they will at the same time become more understanding and accepting of others.

It can be difficult to understand the nature of the three central conditions and the relationship between them. Trainee counsellors can often find it hard to separate them and see that they are both separate and at the same time are very closely interrelated. Each of the conditions is important in its own right but none of them can work on their own. This can sometimes lead beginning counsellors to feel they have to be all three conditions to the same level at the same time. In all my years of practising as a counsellor, I have never been able to achieve that – it does not seem humanly possible. Neither do I think that my clients need that from me. Sometimes my client will need to experience more of my acceptance, at other times he or she will need to experience more of my empathy or more of my authenticity. What I have to do is to try to work out which of those conditions my client needs to experience in that moment that I am with them, as a result of how I am experiencing the client, in that moment in time.

Therapeutic intent

As a counsellor, I believe it is very important to identify as early as possible what it is my client wants from me, in order to enable them to become more fully functioning. As I have said above, I don't believe it is possible to be, and to communicate, all three of the central conditions for therapeutic growth at the same level at the same time. I see that as an ideal which I want to aim at and am unlikely ever to achieve. My sense is that, at any one time, my client will need to experience more of one of the conditions than another. What I need to be able to do is to determine which of the three central conditions my client needs to experience more of, at any time in the relationship. I have learned to think of this as my '*therapeutic intent*'. At any time I need to be considering, 'What is my therapeutic intent with this client? What do they most need to experience in me, at this time?' I then need to work on allowing that aspect of myself to come to the fore and to pay attention to how effective this is for my client. Importantly, I do not want to do this in any mechanistic manner, like a technique. I want it to be largely intuitive and an integrated part of the way that I am.

In this more legalistic and litigious time, I may need to be able to explain why I did what I did as a counsellor and I think that developing an awareness of my therapeutic intent can be really helpful. This does of course take us into the field of assessment and diagnosis, on which Rogers had some important and distinctive views. I will return to this in Chapter 3.

Short-term or time-limited counselling

One of the myths about the person-centred approach is that it is only usable in long-term counselling and that it is not effective in short-term or time-limited work. I want to dispute this strongly, particularly on the basis that Rogers saw the approach as 'a way of being'. He stressed the importance of developing empathy, unconditional positive regard and authenticity, as essential characteristics in the personality of the counsellor and that they should be experienced at least to a minimal degree by the client. If these characteristics are strongly present in the counsellor, I see no reason why they should not be effective in short-term therapy. In my case, I don't believe I need to *be* any different in short-term work, though I may need to *do* some things differently. First and foremost, I do need to be clear and to be explicit with my client, that we will do what we can in the time we have available, which may be less than we might do in longer-term therapy.

I wrote in Chapter 1 about how hard it is to establish and maintain psychological contact at a meaningful level. In short-term work, I need to remind myself of this and to be aware of the ethical issue of getting too deeply involved with a client, in short-term work. It would be unethical to enable a client to go too deeply into significant emotional or psychological issues that they will not be able to resolve in, for example, five or six sessions. Neither do I think it is possible to short-cut the flowing process of the seven stages of therapy referred to earlier. This brings me back again to my concept of *therapeutic intent*. What is it my client most needs from me that can be achieved in the time we have available? My experience has been that above all else in short-term therapy, my client needs to feel accepted, heard and understood from within their own frame of reference. If my client can experience that with me in six sessions, then that in itself will be healing and may provide a platform for them continuing to work on their issues on their own, after short-term therapy is over.

Another idea that I have is that perhaps the key to working as a person-centred counsellor in short-term therapy might lie in the modification of the communication of one or other of those three central conditions. I have a sense that one of the ways in which I work is with the use of 'evocative empathy'. As a counsellor, I work hard to get an accurate sense of how my client experiences their feelings and communicate that to them through tentative empathic clarification. Usually, when I am really accurate at communicating that, somehow it takes my client down to their deeper feelings that may have been out of their awareness, or hidden to them at that time. Sometimes it feels like my deeper empathy somehow evokes deeper feelings in my client, or at the very least opens up access to those deeper, perhaps hidden, feelings. In short-term work I have learned to modify or moderate the communication of my empathic understanding of how my client experiences their feelings. By doing this, I think I can avoid evoking deeper feelings in my client that we will not have time to work with in short-term therapy. It is important to stress that I do not want to be any less empathic; I just need to be careful about the degree to which I communicate my empathy to the client. As a consequence, I think person-centred counsellors can work very effectively in short-term or time-limited counselling, staying true to those necessary and sufficient conditions, without being drawn to use cognitive behavioural or other techniques.

A link to the next chapter

In the next chapter, I will look at beginning the counselling relationship and how the six conditions can be established. I will look more deeply at the first of the six conditions and its relationship to the other five conditions and how they are rooted in some of the fundamental beliefs about human nature. I will also explore how a client and I experienced psychological contact in our work together and touch briefly on the dangers inherent in working at psychological depth with a client.

Recommended reading

Bozarth, Jerold D. and Wilkins, Paul (eds) (2001) *Unconditional Regards.* In the Rogers' Therapeutic Conditions: Evolution, Theory and Practice Series, edited by Gill Wyatt. Ross-on-Wye: PCCS Books.

Rogers, Carl (1990) 'Therapist's view of the good life: the fully functioning person', in Howard Kirschenbaum and Valerie Land Henderson (eds), *The Carl Rogers Reader.* London: Constable, Chapter 27.

Levitt, Bryan E. (2005) *Embracing Non-Directivity: Reassessing Person-centred Theory and Practice in the 21st Century.* Ross-on-Wye: PCCS Books.

Barrett-Lennard, Godfrey T. (2003) *Steps on a Mindful Journey: Person-centred Expressions.* Ross-on-Wye: PCCS Books.

Gillon, E. (2007) *Person-centred Counselling Psychology: an Introduction.* London: Sage.

THREE

Beginning the Counselling Relationship

In this chapter, I will focus on the first stages of developing a therapeutic relationship with a client through the establishing of the six necessary and sufficient conditions for therapeutic growth. I will focus particularly on the importance of the first condition, *psychological contact*, its relationship to the other five conditions and the importance of assessing the potential to establish psychological contact with a client. I will also show how the experiencing of the three central conditions can be really helpful in establishing psychological contact and beginning the counselling relationship. Through some further exploration of the fundamental beliefs about human nature, I will look more closely at how counsellors can prepare themselves to work with their clients in this way. I will also touch briefly on the counsellor's ethical responsibility to assess the client's suitability for counselling and the counsellor's competence to work with each client, and will briefly describe my experience of psychological contact with a client.

The importance of the relationship in counselling

When Carl Rogers first began to develop the person-centred approach, he made it very clear that the most significant difference between the person-centred approach and other approaches was the importance of the counselling relationship. This relationship is based on mutuality, in which both counsellor and client are of equal importance, a relationship in which both parties want to be, and to engage in, with each other. He believed that the relationship forms the context for the presence of the other necessary and sufficient conditions for therapeutic growth, which enable positive personality change to take place. He also made it clear that he believed that all six conditions are closely linked to each other and that, together with a fundamental belief in the actualising tendency in all human beings, they make up the whole of the person-centred approach.

Psychological contact – the essential first condition

Throughout all his writings and in his practice as a counsellor, Rogers placed huge importance on the relationship between the counsellor and the client, even declaring his belief that the relationship is the therapy. He suggested that the existence of this relationship, even in its most minimal form, was the precondition for therapy taking place – without the relationship there could be no therapy. In saying this, he also made it clear that the first condition (the counsellor and the client should be in psychological contact) is absolutely central to the person-centred approach and that the value of the other five conditions is dependent on the presence of that first condition. It could perhaps be better described as a *precondition*, without which therapy is not taking place.

For Rogers, it was very clear that the therapeutic relationship begins with the establishing of the first condition of psychological contact. When he first wrote about this, he used the term 'two persons are in contact' (Rogers, 1957: 95–103). Some two years later he extended this to read 'psychological contact' (Rogers, 1959). He described psychological contact as occurring when both counsellor and client each make some noticeable difference in the experiential field of the other – that in some way, however minimal, each person has some perceived effect on the other person. I take this to mean that in being in the room with my client, the way that I am has some effect on how my client feels, which they are aware of, and also that the way my client is with me has some impact on how I feel, which I am aware of. Rogers also suggested that the counselling relationship was no different from any other relationship and that psychological contact could only occur if both parties had an intention and a willingness to be in contact with each other.

What follows from this is that just because two people are seated in a room and one of them is called a counsellor and the other is called a client, it doesn't mean to say that counselling is actually taking place, even if that is what is supposed to be happening. Any one of a number of other things could be happening, which may be supportive or even therapeutic, helpful or otherwise.

In recent years, I have become even more aware that there have been many times when I was aware that I wasn't really 'counselling' a client. Somehow, for whatever reason, the client and I were not really able to engage. There really did not seem to be any psychological contact present. At the same time, what I was doing seemed to be therapeutic and helpful to the client. I suppose I felt that I was 'working in a counselling way' or even 'using counselling skills', even though I wasn't actually counselling! Because I so dislike the notion of counselling 'skills', which seems so antithetical to the person-centred philosophy, I have taken to referring to this work as '*psycho-social educational support*'.

The importance of wanting to be there

In the person-centred approach, for counselling to actually be taking place, the first of the six necessary and sufficient conditions for therapeutic change must be present. In order for that psychological contact to take place, both individuals must want to be there and to be prepared to engage with each other. Rogers wrote: 'The first condition specifies that a minimal relationship, a psychological contact, must exist. I am hypothesizing, that significant personality change does not occur except in a relationship' (Rogers, 1957: 96). This seems a rather strong hypothesis to make and I suspect that what he meant was, 'personality change does not occur except in a relationship in which psychological contact is present'.

The following example from my practice illustrates this.

A young, male client, Robert, who was about 18 years old, clearly demonstrated the importance of the client wanting to be there and the consequences if they do not. He arrived looking rather down and anxious and seemed a bit suspicious of me. After I had welcomed him and completed the introductory part of the first session, telling him about how I work as a counsellor, outlining how we might work together and the purpose and the boundaries of the counselling relationship, he seemed to be sitting rather stiffly upright in his chair and looked very uncomfortable, with his teeth and hands firmly clenched. He then began to tell me that he had been having a lot of trouble at home and that his parents had insisted that he go for counselling or he would have to leave home.

'So you've been sent for counselling and feel pretty resentful about that?' I asked. 'Yes,' he replied, 'and I really don't want to be here – but I don't feel I have any option.' Robert went on to say, 'If I don't come and see you, they'll kick me out and I'll end up living on the streets because I don't earn enough to get a place of my own. I really don't want to live there with them anymore, but they won't help me to find a place of my own. They just want me to stay there and behave how they want me to.'

I responded by checking out my perception of how he was feeling, 'It sounds like you feel really angry with them and that you are really fed up, and kind of trapped and powerless. Like they've got you on a lead and they won't let go?'

He nodded quietly and said, 'Yes, that is how I feel and I really don't want to talk about it. I just want you to tell me what to do.' Then he sat back in the chair and just looked at me, waiting for me to reply.

I paused and responded by gently reminding him that I had said earlier that I could not and would not tell him what to do, that I had not got any solutions for his problems. I said that I really could understand how angry and let down by his parents he felt, and I could also understand him wanting someone like me to sort it out for him. I also said that I felt pretty powerless and a bit frustrated that I couldn't actually tell him what to do or sort his problems out for him.

He sat silent, looking a little confused, so I wondered out loud to him if he had a feeling that his parents had sent him to me so that I could sort him out for them? At this point he nodded quietly in agreement, looking at me through half-closed eyelids, with a serious expression on his face.

I quietly made it clear that I wasn't there to sort him out or to fix things for his parents, or to find solutions for his problems. All I could do was to offer him a safe place to explore those angry, hurt feelings and that through this process he might be able to decide what it was he really wanted to do. He came back very strongly to say again that he did not want to talk about his feelings. He did not want to be there and he just wanted some answers to his problem. He sat back again, looking at me in a way that seemed very antagonistic and defiant.

Assessing the relationship

It was very clear that we had met and that we were in contact but there seemed no way of developing a relationship with Robert. It just did not seem possible that we could begin counselling when he was so opposed to being there. I felt a bit frustrated and rather sad so I told him this, as well as saying that I fully accepted that he did not want to be sent to see me and that he did not really want to be there. I also said that I could understand him being angry with me because I would not tell him what to do, and that I was OK about that too. I told him that counselling could not work unless he really wanted to be there and that it must be his choice to stay. I wondered out loud to him whether he could actually choose to be there because he wanted to and because he felt it might be useful?

He sat for a while in silence and then said quietly, 'No, this is not for me, I just want some advice.' Then he sat back in silence again.

After a while I said, 'It is very clear to me that we are not going to be able to work together in counselling and I am sad and I am OK about that. It feels like it is your choice.' He nodded quietly in affirmation, so I went on to say, 'I am concerned about your situation though, and the fact that your parents have threatened to kick you out if you don't have counselling. Therefore, would it be helpful if I give you some contact numbers of a couple of organisations that might be able to give you some direct advice and may even be able to help you to find some accommodation you can afford?'

He sat up quickly and smiled, 'That's exactly what I want! If you can do that, I'll even tell my parents what a good counsellor you are!' So I provided him with some contact numbers and told him that if he ever did feel like he wanted to talk with me he could telephone and make an appointment. He left, not looking quite so down as he had when he arrived.

For most of that session we were in contact of some sort, two people in a room talking. He did not want to be there and I did not want to work with him if he did not want to be there. The situation prevented any psychological contact occurring.

Perhaps in those last few moments of our conversation, there was a glimmer of psychological contact happening. He clearly was having some kind of effect on how I was feeling and I clearly had an effect on how he was feeling. Not enough though to bring us together in a sustainable counselling relationship at that time. I said earlier that in trying to start any relationship we have to do things to make it happen. Clearly, in this case my client was not prepared to do anything to enable the relationship to begin. Despite my best efforts with him we did not get started. Afterwards, I explored with my supervisor if there was anything I could have done differently but it did not seem like there was.

Confirmation of research findings

My work with Robert confirmed three important things for me that seem so intrinsic to the importance that Rogers placed on the therapeutic relationship. The first is about the importance of the relationship, the second is about the importance of the client's willingness to engage and the third is their readiness to change. More recently, this has been confirmed by Mick Cooper (2008a). In writing about research into the effectiveness of therapy, he concluded that a key element in the likelihood that therapy would be effective is the willingness of the client to change. He suggests that the quality of the therapeutic relationship is closely associated with the outcomes of therapy and, in particular, the strength of the extent to which counsellor and client agree and collaborate on the goals and tasks of therapy has consistently been shown to relate to effective therapeutic outcomes. Cooper (2008b: 12) also stated: 'the key predictor of outcomes remains the extent to which the client is willing and able to make use of whatever the therapist provides'.

An example of the early experiencing of the central conditions

Another example will serve to show how important the early experiencing of unconditional acceptance, empathy and genuineness can be in establishing psychological contact and beginning the counselling relationship.

A 32-year-old woman called Mary came to see me after her GP suggested that she go for counselling, following an unsuccessful suicide attempt. After the first part of the session, she began to tell me her story of a life in which she had experienced a continuing series of traumatic setbacks and difficulties.

In Mary's early childhood her parents split up and she spent much of her childhood years shuttling backwards and forwards between them. Having to change school frequently, she often found herself being picked on and bullied at each new school. At nine years of age Mary was sent to live with her grandparents, whom she adored. Not long after she moved in, her grandmother died and she was put into care with a number of different foster parents. In one of those homes she was sexually abused by the foster parents' eldest son. In her mid-teens she had been diagnosed as dyslexic and found this really hard to accept. However, she worked hard to overcome this and was able to get enough GCSEs and A Levels to go to university.

In her late teens Mary became pregnant and had to have an abortion. She then found herself in a series of abusive relationships of one form or another and made her first suicide attempt. This led to her dropping out of university.

Once again, she worked hard to overcome her difficulties and managed to get promotion to quite a senior position in a finance company. During this time she had married and then three years ago her husband was killed in a car accident. She had been pregnant at the time and as a result of the accident she had a miscarriage. Her despair led her to make the second unsuccessful suicide attempt.

After a short stay in hospital and a period of time on anti-depressant medication, Mary started again and threw herself back into her work, achieving further promotion to a very senior position. A few months ago she decided to try to make contact again with her parents and had managed to trace them both. To her dismay, neither of them wanted to have any contact with her at all. In fact, they both wanted to deny that she was their daughter. Just after she received that news from them, suddenly and without any warning, she was made redundant by her employers. This then led her to her third suicide attempt.

She drew to a halt and said to me, 'Killing myself would be a blessed relief. It would mean that this can't go on happening any more. I've tried and failed to kill myself three times now. So I know what I did wrong and I now know how to do it right. If I do it again, I won't fail.'

I sat, feeling stunned by the enormity of the setbacks this woman had experienced and said, 'Mary, I am staggered by what you have lived through. You seem to have had the misfortune of a dozen people in your life. It feels like, as you look back at your life all you can see is unhappiness. Like a plain of dried dung punctuated by heaps of drying manure. Every time you start to get things right another pile gets dropped on you and its just happened again with two piles this time.'

She sat nodding quietly and I then said, 'Well I can really understand how that could make you feel like you don't want to go on living. How it makes you feel that you just want to end it all. You feel that it is so unfair this happening to you every time and it is like you feel that it is never going to change and you are forever going to be drowned in piles of steaming dung. I think that if I had experienced all that stuff, I'd probably feel like killing myself too. I think I really understand why you want to kill yourself and I'm not going to try to persuade you not to.' I paused and then added, 'I'll be really sad if you do kill yourself – but I'd understand why.'

We spent the rest of the session exploring her feelings of hurt and despair at all the loss and rejection she had experienced. At the end of the session I asked her if she felt the session had been helpful and if she would like to come and see me again. Her reply rather surprised me.

'Well most of it has been like lots of the people I've talked to and doesn't make a lot of difference really. One thing though, you are the first person who has ever told me it is OK for me to feel as bad as I do. You're the first one who hasn't told me to be positive, to look on the bright side – that I shouldn't feel like this. You're the first one who seems to really understand just how bad it feels for me and that there is nothing wrong with how bad I feel and wanting to kill myself. You really are accepting of me, just as I am and not wanting me to be different in any way.'

She made another appointment to come and see me and that was the beginning of a lengthy counselling relationship. It underlines the importance of really listening in an empathic way, accepting the client's experiencing of her reality and being totally non-judgemental about her, and demonstrates the establishment of psychological contact through those conditions.

The sixth condition

This example also seems to me to illustrate the importance of the sixth condition, 'The communication of the therapist's empathic understanding and unconditional positive regard is to a minimal degree achieved'. Mary really felt accepted, heard and understood in a way she wasn't being by all the people who mattered to her. It doesn't matter how hard I work at being accepting and empathic, if my client doesn't experience that.

Preparing to see clients

Counselling is actually hard, demanding work and it is important to be in the right state of mind for each client you see. Like any good counsellor, I prepare myself for each session with a client, checking that I am ready and willing to work with the client I am about to see. For any counsellor about to begin work with a new client, it is necessary to think about how they are going to be with the client, how they think the client is likely to experience them at this time and to think about what they need to do in establishing initial contact with the client in order to be able to develop and maintain psychological contact and a therapeutic relationship.

Being real and self-accepting

It is here that the process can appear to become rather complicated because of the integrated nature of the six conditions. It can seem almost impossible to completely separate them out from each other. The conditions are separated and individual and yet they are so closely interrelated that they are almost inseparable. If I am going to establish contact with my client, how can I best do that in a way that is not threatening or inappropriate and in a way that is not untrue to the way that I normally am when meeting people? I do not want to play the role of counsellor, wearing a metaphorical mask and costume. While I want to be experienced as a professional, I also want to be experienced as me – as a warm, accepting, empathic individual who is able to be real and present in the relationship.

It is important to remember that Rogers never laid down any blue-prints or tablets of stone about how we should each be in enabling our clients to experience those six conditions with us. He gave no simple rules to abide by, no patterns of words or structures and stages that we should follow. Instead, he indicated that we should be ourselves, we should trust in our intuition and that the most important place for us to experience those conditions was within and from ourselves. If we cannot be unconditionally accepting of ourselves, if we cannot have an accurate sense of how we ourselves are feeling, if we cannot be genuine and undefended with ourselves, how can we really be any of those things with other people?

Being yourself

Rogers did not say: 'Be like me', 'Do it this way', 'Say this', 'Don't say that' or 'Use this technique or that method'. What he did was to identify the importance of each of us developing the central conditions of the person-centred approach, in each of us, in our own way. Because of that, it is not possible to say how anyone else should meet and establish contact with their clients. How each of us does that with each client that we meet will be different to some degree. However, I can describe the way that I do it which seems to work for me and for my clients.

Remembering the basic beliefs

Before meeting any new client, I find it useful to remind myself of my basic person-centred beliefs about the nature of human beings. My belief that however stressed or distressed my client may be, however unhappy or damaged they may be, however difficult it may be for them to function fully as a human being, all human beings have an inborn tendency to grow and develop, to maintain and to enhance themselves. This is true, even in the worst conditions human beings may find themselves in, they will always seek to do more than just survive. The choice between self-actualisation and self-destruction is guided by this directional tendency and I must remember to trust in that individual positive directional tendency in my client.

Rogers believed that this positive directional tendency could only really be thwarted by death. I need to remember also that Rogers saw this self-actualising tendency in individuals as part of an overall formative tendency in the universe, present in all living things. That tendency can clearly be diverted or distorted as a result of the painful, cruel or traumatic experiences of life. At the same time, the experiencing of those conditions of genuineness, warm acceptance and empathic understanding in the counselling relationship can enable an individual to restore and revitalise their drive towards self-actualisation and to seize the opportunity to be a fully functioning person. I need to remind myself that despite whatever my client may present, they are a real, live human being, with immense potential.

From that central position of belief in the positive nature of the directional drive of human beings, I also need to remind myself of another important perspective about people and about my role as counsellor. The person-centred approach has a strong belief that each of us is the only expert in our own internal world. I am the only one who really knows how I feel, the only one who knows how I experience myself and the world around me. The only person I could possibly be an expert on is me. I may have a lot of experience and knowledge, a lot of insight and self-awareness and even some wisdom, but I must remember that my client is the only one who knows themselves, what feelings they experience and how they experience them, and their world with themselves in it. In preparing myself for my first session with a client, I want to make myself ready to really hear, understand and accept how they experience themselves, the world that they inhabit and their issues and concerns in that world.

Counsellors' experiencing of the central conditions in themselves

I have discovered that in order to experience the central conditions in myself, in the brief period before the client arrives, I need to begin by checking that I am being accepting, empathic and genuine towards myself. I need to really check out how I am feeling in myself and how I am feeling about the work I am about to do. If I can then be ready to be accepting, empathic and genuine, which includes being prepared to be open with my feelings with my client, in a way that feels natural and comfortable for me, then it is likely that we will move fairly quickly from just meeting, to beginning to have psychological contact and the start of a relationship.

In meeting new clients I know that as with meeting any new people, I am always a little nervous. I have a slight, incipient shyness which has remained in me since my adolescence and which I have actually learned to value and respect. It is an element of my personality that has been quite useful for me at times. I have learned that if I deny my nervousness at meeting new people, it will usually find a way of showing itself and usually makes things worse for me and for them. At the same time, I want to check that it is only my usual shyness at meeting new people that I am feeling and that I really do want to meet and work with this new client. I have learned that it is really useful for me to be aware of those feelings of slight nervousness at meeting a new client and to be transparent with those feelings, as I was with the client I described at the start of Chapter 1. I want to do that in a way which is natural for me and does not make the client feel that I do not want to see them or that they are to blame for my nervousness. I also want it to be experienced by the client as making it all right for them to feel nervous too.

In those early moments of meeting and greeting the client, I want to get a sense of who and how they are, without making assumptions or interpretations based on the way they present themself to me. I want to avoid making judgements about the kind of person they are, based on the clothes they are wearing, how they talk or the way they look. I also want to be experienced as accepting and gently empathic in those early moments. I know that for many clients, coming to see a counsellor for the first time can be a very scary experience and it can take a long time and a lot of courage to turn up for that first appointment. Sometimes, being too empathic or too accurate with empathy in the early stages, before the relationship has actually formed, can be very unsettling for a client and can sometimes drive them away. By being too empathic too soon, my client may feel that I can see right through them, that there is nothing they can hide and this will prevent them from developing a trust in me. They may feel very unsafe and unprotected or perhaps even that they are being forced to face up to feelings they may not yet have acknowledged. So I need to remember to be tentative and sensitive with my empathic clarification in the beginning of the relationship and to work patiently towards a point where my client can experience my full empathy without fear.

So, by being gently and appropriately transparent with my feelings, in the moment, I will enable my client to experience my genuineness in a non-threatening way. By checking out how my client feels about being there with me and how they feel about all the things they are telling me, and tentatively communicating my understanding of those feelings, I will enable my client to feel heard and understood. By listening in a calm attentive and accepting manner I will enable my client to experience my unconditional regard for them. I want to do all of these things as soon as I possibly can in meeting the client and engaging with them and their concerns.

Assessment and establishing psychological contact

While I want to begin building the relationship right from my first contact with the client, at the same time I need to take responsibility for clarifying the nature of the counselling relationship. In meeting a client for the first time, as well as making it possible for us to establish psychological contact and to engage with each other, I also have an ethical responsibility to assess the appropriateness of us working together and my competence to work with this particular client.

In my private practice as a person-centred counsellor, I would not carry out a detailed, formal assessment and diagnosis of a client, and I certainly would not usually use an assessment form, although in many Health Service settings I may have to find a way to do that which fits with my approach. As we move towards regulation of the counselling profession, it is likely that all counsellors will be required to carry out a careful assessment of each client's needs and to work with the client to produce a formulation of how the counsellor and client are going to work together and what the client wants to achieve. *The Ethical Framework* (BACP, 2010) makes it clear that I have an ethical responsibility to engage in explicit contracting with each of my clients before counselling begins, so that I can make an informed decision that I am competent to work with a client and that the client can make an informed decision that they are likely to be able to benefit from counselling with me. I really like to try to be in a position with my client so that we can both be able to make our decision on the appropriateness of working together, by the end of the first session if at all possible. For me, this forms an important element of the process of moving from just meeting, to establishing psychological contact between us and the development of a therapeutic relationship.

Maintaining psychological contact

Although it can be very difficult to attain, it is really important to try to establish some level of psychological contact in first meeting the client and to work hard at strengthening and deepening that condition throughout the counselling relationship. I need to continue to work at maintaining that contact at the start of and throughout every session I have with the client. I cannot afford to just be in the room and just listen to my client – any friend or acquaintance can do that. I need to continue to do all the things I have described above, which enable me to establish psychological contact in the first place, in order to maintain it. This is hard work and can be emotionally and sometimes physically exhausting. In order to be able to work in this demanding way, I need to take good care of myself, both physically and emotionally, and also to monitor my effectiveness and my continuing health through the regular use of supervision. Most of all, I need to ensure that I can be in psychological contact with myself, so that I can experience the central conditions within and from myself.

Psychological contact in short-term and long-term person-centred counselling

Working over quite a lengthy period of time gives a continuing opportunity for the depth and strength of the counselling relationship to develop and be maintained. In many settings, longer-term counselling is becoming something of a luxury, particularly in more recent times when short-term therapy has become more favoured for financial reasons. Sometimes it has been suggested that the person-centred approach will only work in long-term counselling. I do not believe that to be true. Clearly, for some clients and for some deep-seated issues and concerns, therapy may need to be a lengthy process, continuing for as much as two, three or even more years. For some clients, shorter periods of time may be appropriate and acceptable. There is no simple rule of thumb that can determine how long counselling should go on for. It is possible, with hard work, commitment and application by the counsellor, for therapeutic presence to be developed within any counselling relationship, whether it is a short-term or long-term one. A key feature of the applicability of the person-centred approach is the willingness of the counsellor to work really hard at developing and maintaining the six necessary and sufficient conditions within themselves, along with developing the capacity to communicate these in an integrated way through the counsellor's therapeutic presence, in relating in depth with clients. It is clearly true that this may be more difficult in short-term work and counsellors should exercise some care and caution about entering into a deep relationship with a client whom they may only be able to see for a short and limited number of sessions. Doing so and ending after only six sessions might leave a client feeling very vulnerable or even rejected or abandoned.

Establishing psychological contact is a sophisticated process which I believe is difficult to establish and maintain at any meaningful level. As I have said earlier in this chapter, Rogers did not give any detailed explanation of the concept, other than to say that in some way both counsellor and client have some perceived effect on each other.

My experience as a counsellor, supervisor and trainer has led me to develop a view that significant psychological contact is very hard to establish and maintain and it may take somewhere between 10 and 20 sessions to achieve this. It can be experienced fleetingly in a first session with a client and in brief deeper moments in the early weeks of developing a relationship. The experiencing of deep psychological contact is, I believe, not the most common experience for counsellors because it involves both counsellor and client in taking the risk of engaging at psychological depth with each other. It is also very hard to describe what this demanding experience is like. One of the experiences I have had might help to illuminate this.

I recall working with a man in his late twenties, who had been coming to see me for almost three months with some distressing symptoms of depression. We seemed to have developed a reasonably trusting relationship, although for most of the time Michael seemed to be telling me the latest chapter of the story of his life. He seemed very unwilling to be in touch with his feelings or to explore them. I continued to work very acceptingly with him, patiently trying to encourage him to be with his feelings. Then, in the 14th session, I became aware of just how frustrated I was feeling and took the risk of being transparent with this, as he finished reporting to me the latest events in his life.

I started by saying: 'Michael, I wonder if we could pause for a moment while I share with you something that I am feeling at the moment?' He looked at me seeming to wonder where I was going with this.

'It sounds like some really important things happened last week that I imagine might have been quite painful for you and yet you haven't given me any sense of what your feelings about them were? You've just told me another part of your story, kind of reporting back to me what has happened in the last week, almost like reading a newspaper article about it.'

I continued, 'I guess I'm feeling pretty frustrated and a bit inadequate, that somehow, I can't find the way to enable you to really let me know how you feel about these things that are happening to you. I'm a bit frustrated with what is happening, and I'm really frustrated with me. I'm wondering if it is possible for you to be here with your feelings rather than just telling me the story?' I'm also wondering if there is anything you think I can do to help with that?'

He sat in silence for a while with a puzzled expression on his face and then said, 'You mean you want me to do what you just did? Say what I'm feeling right here and now?'

I just looked back with an accepting smile on my face and nodded quietly. Then, slowly, haltingly he began to engage with his feelings and to share them in a way that he had never done before.

I suddenly felt that I was in a very different place, like we were in a sort of 'time warp' where time had stood still, even our very surroundings seemed to have just disappeared. There was just Michael and me and his feelings, in a way that had not happened before. This almost unreal state continued for a further 30 minutes of deep engagement.

Towards the end of the session Michael let go of his feelings and started to talk in a more story-telling way.

At the end of the session, as I always do with my clients, I asked him for some feedback on how the session had been for him, if there was anything particularly useful in it or anything he would have liked me to do differently.

He replied, 'Well there was that bit where you made it seem different by telling me how you were feeling. I thought you were telling me off at first, then I realised you weren't. I don't know what happened then, but it felt like..... Hmm, I don't know how to describe it..... It was like..... well.... you know when you sit in a church on your own and it feels like a huge and quiet and special space..... Well it felt like I was in a place like that. There was just me and you in this place and I felt very safe and very scared at the same time. I felt I could tell you anything and all of a sudden my feelings were just there and you really seemed to get how I was feeling and it was all right for me to have those feelings.'

I replied, 'Yes, it felt kind of special for me too, like we really met each other.'

We quietly made our next appointment and I wondered if we would be able to get back to that place again and what I would need to do (or rather how I would need to be) to enable that to happen.

In the above instance, the key to movement in that therapeutic relationship as always resulted from two things. The first of these was really being internally congruent. Being fully aware of how I was feeling in the moment. The second was being prepared to take the risk of being transparent with those feelings to my client.

Ethical considerations and challenges

There are, of course, significant ethical dangers in establishing psychological contact and a close relationship. It will be easy for both counsellor and client to misunderstand the feelings that arise in such a caring relationship. It is therefore essential that counsellors pay attention to these possible dangers and actively concentrate on maintaining their adherence to the ethical principles fundamental to counselling, and work hard at all times to maintain appropriate boundaries. I believe it is important to avoid any physical demonstrations of affection to my clients, and in fact to avoid touching them unless for client safety reasons I have to. This is important because I can never know how my client may experience me touching them, or what they may read into it. I must also avoid entering into any other kind of relationship with my clients, outside therapy, even when therapy has finished. For me, I do want my warmth, acceptance and empathy to be experienced by my client and at the same time I need both of us to remember that this is a 'professional' relationship. Regular supervision is essential to enable a counsellor to manage clear and explicit boundaries and to ensure that their work is always ethically proper.

A link to the next chapter

In the next chapter I will further explore the relationship between the three central conditions, particularly in relation to authenticity and how challenging this work can be. I will use examples to show how, by being both genuine and present in the counselling relationship, the counsellor helps the client to recognise and challenge some of the unconscious processes which are occurring within the client. I will briefly explore the importance of the careful observation of what the client does and says, the non-judgemental communication of this to the client and the avoidance of interpretation by the counsellor. I will look at the importance of establishing and maintaining appropriate boundaries in the relationship, including a reminder of the importance of maintaining what Rogers called the 'as if' quality of empathy (Rogers, 1959). I will end the next chapter with a brief look at the broader applications of the person-centre approach, beyond counselling.

Recommended reading

Casemore, R. (2001) *Surviving Complaints against Counsellors and Psychotherapists: Understanding and Healing the Hurt.* Ross-on Wye: PCCS Books.

Rogers, Carl (1990) 'The characteristics of a helping relationship', in Howard Kirschenbaum and Valerie Land Henderson (eds), *The Carl Rogers Reader.* London: Constable, Chapter 8.

Cooper, M. (2008) *Essential Research Findings in Counselling and Psychotherapy: the Facts are Friendly.* Lutterworth: BACP and Sage.

Vincent, S. (2005) *Being Empathic: a Companion for Counsellors and Therapists.* Abingdon: Radcliffe.

FOUR

The Challenge of the Three Central Conditions

In this chapter I will begin by further clarifying my understanding of what I have termed the three central conditions. I will then explore the challenging nature of the person-centred approach to counselling and the concept of authenticity. I will also indicate the importance of being phenomenological through the careful observation of what the client does and says, the non-judgemental communication of the counsellor's experiencing of these phenomena to the client and the avoidance of interpretation by the counsellor. I will look at the ethical imperative of 'self-respect' or 'self-care' and, linked to this, the importance of establishing and maintaining appropriate boundaries in the relationship. I will also look briefly at the wider applications of the person-centred approach, beyond counselling. I will begin with a brief explanation of my current understanding of what I refer to as the three central conditions.

The three central conditions – condition 3

The second person, whom we shall term the therapist, is congruent or integrated in the relationship.

Originally, Rogers talked about the need for the counsellor to be congruent in him or her self and in the relationship, as a fundamental basis for the best communication (Rogers, 1961). In later life, he began to use the term 'real' (Rogers, 1980) and later still, the term 'authentic' as more accurately describing what he meant (Rogers, 1970). I see authenticity as being made up of two elements: congruence, which is an internal condition, and appropriate transparency, which is the outward expression of those internal feelings. The ability to be congruent is the ability to have a match between how we are feeling and how we are being. Transparency is best defined as talking about or in other ways showing the feelings that are being experienced in the counsellor. Rogers believed it was important for the counsellor to be really in touch with their own feelings as they are experiencing them and to be prepared to be with those feelings as they occur in the counselling relationship, in an open and undefended way.

The three central conditions – condition 4

The therapist experiences unconditional positive regard for the client.

Rogers suggested that healthy psychological growth in a client will happen when the counsellor establishes a safe and permissive relationship which allows clients to fully express their feelings (Rogers, 1961). In this relationship, the counsellor must 'prize' or value the individual as a unique being who has the capacity to determine what their problems are and the ability to identify and choose appropriate solutions to enable them to become more fully functioning. The counsellor must accept and be non-judgemental about the client's feelings in order to enable the client to feel fully accepted and free from all pressure. Rogers believed that if the client was truly able to feel accepted by the counsellor, this would enable the client to become more accepting of themselves. He was convinced that each of us has an innate capacity for self-understanding and if unconditionally accepted and provided with a safe space in which to grow, we will begin to develop greater insight into ourselves and a better understanding of the causes and consequences of our behaviour and our feelings. This will lead to us being more in touch with our inner self and less controlled by the thoughts, feelings and words of others. It is useful to remember that Rogers saw complete unconditional positive regard as an ideal to be aimed at and something that was very difficult to achieve. He saw this full acceptance as involving the counsellor's willingness for the client to be whatever immediate feeling was going on in the client. He wrote,

'It is a non-possessive caring. When the therapist prizes the client in a total rather than a conditional way, forward movement is likely' (Rogers, 1967: 304–311). For me, another way of putting this is that I want my clients to feel 'cared about', rather than 'cared for'.

The three central conditions – condition 5

The therapist experiences an empathic understanding of the client's internal frame of reference and endeavours to communicate this experience to the client.

Rogers suggested that this is more than just being able to sense how the other person feels – an attribute that most of us have to some degree (Rogers, 1961). It means the counsellor maintains a continuing interest in and a commitment to understanding how, from moment to moment, the client experiences their feelings from within the client's belief system and context – what is usually called their frame of reference – rather than from that of the counsellor. Also, it is important that the counsellor should be able to tentatively communicate their understanding of the client's feelings in such a way that the client can really experience being heard and understood and not judged. In the early days, Rogers described the process of doing this as 'reflection of feelings' – a term which he later much regretted using. He stated that it was important to avoid the mere reflection or parroting back of feelings, but rather to focus on checking out and clarifying how the client was experiencing their feelings, in order to lead to real understanding of that by the counsellor, and the communicating of it to the client (Rogers, 1986). It seems to me that 'empathic clarification', would be a much more useful term to use as it more clearly describes what Rogers was alluding to.

The first among equals of the three central conditions

There is a sense that each of these three central conditions is of equal importance. Paradoxically, however, I see congruence as *primus inter pares*, the first among equals. Rogers himself made the point that congruence is the basis for being together in a real relationship (Rogers, 1980). I see congruence as an internal state, which can be defined as 'the level of harmony between how an individual is feeling and how they are presenting their feelings, first of all to themselves and then to others'. Someone who feels angry or sad or irritated but presents themselves as being calm and shows no feelings or shows quite different feelings can be said to be in a state of 'incongruence'. Someone who shows their feelings and behaves in a way that corresponds with how they are feeling can be said to be congruent or authentic. Leitaur (1993) takes this further by saying that if we are not open to our own experiencing of ourselves, we can never be really open or empathic to our client's experience.

To be effective, the person-centred counsellor's authenticity, genuineness or realness must be at the highest possible levels. In essence, this depends on the counsellor's capacities for being properly in touch with the complexities of feelings, thoughts and attitudes which they themselves are experiencing as they seek to empathise with and to respond appropriately to the feelings, thoughts and attitudes within their clients, as they are being with the client. The more the counsellor can do this, the more they will be perceived by the client as a person of real flesh and blood who is willing to be seen and known, and not as a clinical professional shielded behind a metaphorical white coat.

The counsellor's transparency is quite a complex issue. Although clients need to experience their counsellor's essential humanity and 'realness', they do not need to have their counsellor's feelings forced down their throat. The counsellor must not only attempt to remain firmly in touch with the flow of their own experience of the client and of themselves, they must also have the discrimination to know when and how to communicate what they are experiencing for the benefit of the client. For this reason, I believe that the two essential elements of transparency are 'immediacy' and 'appropriateness'. Immediacy is in relation to the timeliness of the transparent expression of the counsellor's feelings. Appropriateness is in relation to the level or depth of feelings that the counsellor is being transparent with.

Being internally congruent calls for significant self-awareness on the part of the counsellor. They must work at being as transparent to themselves as they possibly can be, in terms of being in touch with the flow of their own experience of their own feelings during the counselling interview and in the counselling relationship as a whole, with each client with whom they work. This calls for constant vigilance, discipline and very hard work to sense all the feelings that the counsellor can readily be aware of within themselves, at the same time as they are paying full attention to accurately sensing the client's feelings. It will be important for the counsellor to be phenomenological towards themselves in order to notice all the unconscious and conscious behaviours that act as signals of their feelings that may be disguised or hidden from the counsellor. It calls for what I describe as 'my third eye', which sits outside me as I work as a counsellor and in some way monitors how I am being, while I am with my client, without taking any attention away from my client.

In being aware of what is going on inside the counsellor in their way of being, the counsellor must intuitively judge what it is appropriate to reveal to the client, when is the most helpful time to do it and what is the most appropriate way in which to reveal those feelings, that will be helpful for the client, to the relationship and to the counsellor.

It is essential to differentiate between transparency and self-disclosure. Self-disclosure is about telling the client your story, describing your experiences, and should be avoided as much as possible. It can so easily lead to the client seeing the counsellor as playing the game of 'Me too', or even to the roles of counsellor and client becoming reversed within the relationship! Transparency, on the other hand, is about sharing with the client the feelings that the counsellor is experiencing in the relationship, if and when that will be helpful to the client.

Plainly, authenticity and transparency offer the potential for abuse of the client by the counsellor and present real risks if not appropriately applied. As counsellor, I need to be careful in being authentic and present and appropriately transparent, in order not to overwhelm my client or to reverse the tables and turn myself into client and my client into counsellor. Being authentic doesn't mean being in the client's face with my feelings, but carefully choosing what, when and how to share my feelings in a way that is not threatening to the client! On the other hand, I have learned that if I experience feelings in me occurring within the relationship, it is far better and usually more productive to take the risk of expressing those feelings than withholding them, even if I do that in a way that is less appropriate than I might.

Differences in style

Different counsellors will choose to express their authenticity in different ways and different clients will also call for different styles of communicating. Whatever the precise form of their communication, person-centred counsellors will be striving to communicate to their clients an attitude expressive of a desire to be deeply and fully involved in the counselling relationship with their client, without pretence and without the protection of professional impersonality. They will be striving to be genuinely and authentically present and, in doing so, in one sense hopefully modelling how the client might be in the relationship.

Authenticity and challenge – the need for toughness in the counsellor

In my work as a counsellor and as a supervisor of other counsellors, I have been struck, time and again, by a frequently recurring message from clients. Time after time I have heard clients saying that they really wanted to be challenged. They frequently said that they did not want their counsellor to just be a warm, fluffy listener. They really needed their counsellor to engage with them and to be challenging in some way. However, in order for challenge to be accepted, it is essential that the client feels fully accepted.

Being there with all of myself

While it is essential for person-centred counsellors to be experienced as empathic, warm and sensitive, compassionate and caring, we also need to be experienced as more than that. If we offer only those softer, warmer, more sensitive aspects of ourselves in our counselling work, then we will be doing both ourselves and our clients a real disservice. This is particularly true for person-centred counsellors because of the importance of being authentic, being real both in ourselves and with our clients. Put simply, I need to be authentic in the counselling relationship with all of myself, not just with the parts of me that I like.

The importance of challenge and being uncompromising

In 2002, Windy Dryden, Michael Jacobs and I were interviewed on video about our views on congruence, authenticity and appropriate transparency, from the cognitive-behavioural, psychodynamic and person-centred perspectives (Casemore et al., 2002). One of the striking things in that video was that when asked by the interviewer to say something about ourselves, Windy Dryden, Michael Jacobs and I each described ourselves as 'uncompromising individuals'. Each of us said that in addition to seeing ourselves as individuals who can be warm, caring, sensitive and compassionate, we also saw ourselves as having the capacity to be quite tough and uncompromising in our lives and in our work with clients. All three of us saw our work with clients as hugely challenging both for ourselves and for our clients and we each felt that if counselling was not challenging for the client, then it probably would not be of much use to them.

Prizing the client – love and tough love – the power of full acceptance

Carl Rogers suggested that as a client moves from experiencing themselves as an unworthy, unacceptable and unlovable person to the realisation that they are deeply understood and deeply accepted by the counsellor, that this could be experienced by the client as being 'loved' by the counsellor. They could experience being loved in a way that was not sexual, parental or in any way demanding, but loved in a way that gave the client permission to love themselves (Rogers, 1951). What Rogers was talking about was a very special kind of love based on a full acceptance of the individual, that was in itself hugely challenging to the individual. He described it as caring for the client in a non-possessive way, as a separate person who has permission to have their own feelings and their own experiences (Kirschenbaum and Henderson, 1990).

Very few of us experience unconditional love in our upbringing. Most, if not all of us, are brought up to feel that we are unlovable or unacceptable in some way – that we are largely or even totally worthless, unless we do what someone else wants us to do, behave as someone else wants us to behave or become as someone else wants us to become. We are conditioned to believe that we must not do anything which would upset someone else or cause them to think badly of us. We are taught to measure ourselves and our worth by how we sense other people feel about us or might feel about us. If we have that kind of deeply rooted set of beliefs about ourselves, then to experience the counsellor deeply accepting us, deeply accepting and understanding our feelings, believing that we are lovable and worthy, is likely to be hugely challenging to us. It means that almost everything we have been taught about ourselves is untrue, a lie. Clients can find this really hard to believe at first and can be quite thrown by the experience and may disbelieve or even try to reject it and even reject the counsellor.

The experiencing of full acceptance by the client offers two significant opportunities for change. First, the client who experiences full accept-ance may then be able to begin to accept themselves in ways that they have not done before. As a counsellor, I have experienced within my clients and within myself that the more someone tries to change themselves, the more their unconscious internal drives resist change to prevent that from happening. The key to change in the individual is self-acceptance. If, as a consequence of experiencing my full acceptance of them, my client begins to truly and fully accept themselves as they are, then somehow, change will begin to happen in them. Secondly, the more my client experiences my acceptance of them, the more often and the more strongly I am able to challenge them about how I experience the way they are being and enable them to discover the range of choices for being different that are open to them.

An example of the challenge of experiencing acceptance

In previous chapters, some examples of the importance of acceptance in the counselling relationship have been given. A further example will show the challenging nature of this condition for both the counsellor and the client, along with the importance of understanding how it is experienced by the client.

James, in his early thirties, was referred to me for counselling as he was very depressed. He seemed very unhappy and looked very unhealthy. During our first interview he talked in a low monotone, his eyes often welling up with tears though he did not actually cry. I concentrated on listening to him carefully, while he told me that he felt he was a complete failure and that there was nothing about him that was any good. Over the past ten years he had been in a succession of jobs, none of which he seemed able to hang on to for more than a couple of years before he was sacked or made redundant. Six months ago he had been made redundant again from a job he quite liked and felt that he could cope with. Since then he had been totally unsuccessful in finding a new job. Nobody seemed to want to employ him.

In that same monotone, he went on to describe the history of his personal relationships, which seemed to paint a very similar picture to his experiences of failure and rejection in his work. He was the youngest of three children and both of his parents were teachers who had been very committed to their jobs. He said that he knew from a very early age that his parents loved and valued his older brother and sister far more than him. When he was six years old, his mother had told him that he was a mistake. She really had not wanted him at all and that she still did not love him or want him. All through his childhood and adolescence his brother and sister had taunted him with being 'unwanted' and had been very cruel to him. At 18, after a huge row with his father, he left his parents' house and had never been back. Since then he had lived in various different parts of the country and never returned to the town where he was born and brought up. After leaving his parents, he had been in a number of short-term relationships with a succession of women, none of them lasting more than a few months. In each relationship he described himself as being used or abused in some way and that he had never found anyone who seemed able to love him. His latest relationship had ended when his girlfriend walked out the day after he was made redundant, telling him he was a useless failure.

The first communication of acceptance

At this point in his story he stopped talking and seemed to be close to tears. I noticed that he was sat huddled in his chair, staring down at his lap, with his arms wrapped tightly around his body and his legs tightly crossed and tucked under his chair. I gently checked out how he was feeling with the words, 'I get the sense that you're feeling really hurt and alone, quite damaged by all this rejection. I've noticed how you are sitting and I'm wondering if it feels like you're struggling to hold yourself together.' He looked up at me and nodded in agreement. He seemed to stay with those feelings for a while and then went on to say, 'You must think I'm absolutely useless, a complete and utter failure, like there's no point in me being alive?'

I responded by saying. 'No, that's not what I feel, or think, James. I do feel very saddened by the picture you have painted of your experiences. I guess I'm wondering if that is how you feel about yourself?'

He nodded slowly, looking at me with a very sad expression on his face, as I went on to say, tentatively, 'It sounds to me like all of your life you have experienced being rejected, being unloved, being unwanted, being really hurt by nobody ever really caring for you? I'm wondering if you are also starting to feel that it must be your fault, that all of these people who have rejected you can't be wrong – that perhaps you really are unlovable?'

I paused for a moment as he sat, silently looking at me and nodding, as I went on to say, 'I guess I'm also wondering if you are expecting me to reject you too – that I'm not going to want you to be here?'

As he sat there nodding silently, I went on to say, 'Well, I'm not going to reject you if I can possibly help it. I also don't believe that anyone is completely unlovable, completely unacceptable, so I don't believe that about you. I can't undo the damage that has been done to you over the years or take away the pain you are experiencing. What I can try to do is to provide a safe place, here in this relationship, where you can explore all those painful feelings about yourself and all those people who have hurt you in so many different ways, where you can feel really accepted, as you are, and not judged. As long as you want to keep coming to see me, I'll try to be here for you.' He agreed to come and see me again the following week.

The struggle with being accepted

During the next six months James kept coming to see me and really struggled with my acceptance of him. In fact, he made it very clear that he could not believe that I was really accepting him, that it was impossible for anyone to do that. He often seemed to be intent on challenging my acceptance of him by failing to turn up or being late for appointments and behaving in some quite challenging ways during our interviews.

The client's experience of acceptance as not being accepted

On one occasion he said, 'It sort of feels like you are accepting me – but I know that I'm such a failure that you can't really do that. You're only pretending to because you're paid to. You can't really care about me!'

I responded with, 'It sounds like my acceptance of you is a huge challenge and that you have really got to fight against it. It feels to me like you don't know what to do or how to be, if I accept you? I guess I understand you feeling that way, on the basis of your experience of how everyone else has treated you – and you still really expect me to reject you.'

His response really threw me, 'There you are, you see. You don't really accept me; you don't accept that I can't accept you accepting me!'

I puzzled for a moment trying to understand what he had said and slowly realised that he was right. I said, 'Yes, you are right. I've been concentrating hard on being really accepting of you and I've not been accepting that at this moment in time you really aren't able to do that.'

Acceptance as a challenge

He smiled knowingly at me, as though he had won a small victory. I went on to wonder tentatively, 'That must be an incredibly lonely and terrifying place to be, to believe that no one, not even your counsellor, could possibly be accepting and care about you?' Gently but firmly, I continued with, 'I don't want to force you to feel accepted by me, I'm OK about that. In fact there is no way I can force you to do that. You could choose to do it for yourself, when and if you are ready. What I do want to do is to really try to understand what it feels like to be you, in that isolated, lonely place inside you.'

James replied, 'You mean I don't have to feel accepted by you, I don't have to feel you care about me?'

'That's right', I replied in a very accepting tone, 'it's your choice. I'm OK with you choosing to reject my acceptance of you and I'm even OK with you choosing to reject me.'

James left and telephoned later to cancel his next appointment and I did not see him again for several months. When he came back to see me again, very little seemed to have changed for him. He started by telling me how angry he had been with me and that he was really surprised that I was prepared to see him again. He went on to say, 'But then you're pretty tough, aren't you? You'd have to be, to care about someone like me. I was really surprised when you seemed to know

how terrified I felt and even more surprised when you didn't try to
make me feel better. Maybe that was pretty accepting, really – and I
suppose I'm really scared of being accepted as well as of being
rejected.'

I responded by quietly saying, 'And I guess I wonder which of those
is the most frightening for you, the acceptance or the rejection?'

The impact of acceptance on the locus of evaluation

James and I then went on to work with each other for a further two
years, through much of which he really struggled with his fear of being
accepted, which was such a challenge to his deeply held inner belief
that he was completely unacceptable by anyone. The focus of much of
my work as his counsellor was to enable James to change from using
what other people thought and felt about him as the basis for his
evaluation of himself, to an internalised locus of evaluation of himself,
by himself. Through my unconditional acceptance he was able to begin
to be more accepting and loving of himself and to begin to believe that
he was acceptable and lovable by others.

Challenging the self-blaming tendency

There were many times in which I found myself communicating my
empathic understanding of how James felt about himself and at the
same time I was challenging him to recognise that he had been taught
to believe this by significant other people and that he could actually
choose to feel differently about himself, on the basis of how he actually
experienced himself. There were times when it was quite clear that
James really did not like me or my challenging him by showing how I
experienced what he had said. However, he stayed with me and the
challenge seemed to have worked, in that, more and more, he began to
recognise that he did not always have to blame himself when things
went wrong. He began to recognise that when things went wrong, it

was not automatically his fault because he believed he was a failure and unacceptable.

Counselling is hard work

Working with James was a really demanding experience in which he needed me to be very empathic, accepting and sensitive to his needs. At the same time, he really needed me to challenge his experiencing of himself as unlovable, and having no choices. Taking the risk of challenging a client by being appropriately transparent with my feelings and being prepared to say how I am experiencing them, is quite daunting and takes a lot of energy to maintain. It also means I have to be really knowledgeable about myself and to have really worked on maintaining my own emotional and psychological health. In the counselling room there really is no place for me to hide from my client. There is nothing soft and fuzzy about this kind of work. It takes determination, commitment and effort to be there with the whole of myself and not just the parts of me that I approve of.

The locus of evaluation of the counsellor

In working with James, it was very clear that he had been taught to evaluate himself on the basis of how other people felt about him. They felt he was worthless and unlovable and treated him in that way, so he believed that about himself. To work with clients like James, I need to make sure that my locus of evaluation of me is firmly fixed in me. That I am not completely dependent on measuring my effectiveness as a counsellor by how my clients feel about me. I need to be able to work with them, without needing them to like me or only experience me as nice, warm, sensitive and approachable. I need to be able to accept that at times my clients will not like me, that they may sometimes be quite angry with me or with some of the things which I say in challenging them and helping them to discover the choices they have in how they experience themselves and their feelings. I need to be able to be quite tough and uncompromising in my acceptance, my 'love' for my clients. Importantly, that needs to be based in a strong and uncompromising acceptance and love of myself.

Close and at a distance

A helpful process in communicating my prizing of my clients, and in being quite tough in challenging them, is maintaining an appropriate clinical distance in the relationship. This is, after all, a counselling relationship with ethical boundaries that are important to manage. Client and counsellor can experience real intimacy in the counselling relationship, particularly when warmth, strong empathy and unconditional acceptance are felt by the client. Yet this intimacy needs to be different in some important ways from that which might be felt in personal and social relationships. It can be friendly and warm and at the same time it is not a friendship. This is a subtle and difficult difference to understand and to maintain.

I want my client and I to experience closeness based on genuineness, empathy and unconditional acceptance. I want to be able to enter into my client's experiencing of their reality so that I can get a real understanding of how they experience the world of their feelings, from their frame of reference, rather than from mine. At the same time, I do not want to be completely sucked into my client's world of feelings. I need to remain in contact with my own world while experiencing their world as much as possible, without actually being in their internal world. I need to remember that I am the counsellor and that I have the responsibility to manage the boundaries of the relationship and to keep it safe for us both.

The quality of 'as-ifness' in empathy

Carl Rogers identified an important aspect of empathy, which he called 'as-ifness' (Rogers, 1959). This is an important and difficult element of managing the boundaries of the counselling relationship. I need to remember that I am trying to get a real sense of how my client experiences their feelings, from within themselves. That is not about me trying to feel their feelings in the same way that they do, but rather to get a sense of them 'as if' I was in their world, without actually being there. If I enter too fully into my client's feelings and begin to experience them in myself, I will not be treating them as a separate person who has the right to have their own feelings, their own experiences. Rather, I will be identifying too closely with my client and may be experienced as invading them in some way.

Noticing and avoiding interpretation

One aspect of the person-centred approach which is really helpful in staying in touch with your own world of feelings and avoiding becoming over-identified with the client and their feelings is the importance of being phenomenological, a word that is difficult to say and can be hard to understand. Put simply, it means the act of noticing the things that happen in the counselling relationship, without interpreting them or giving them a meaning. It is the process of noticing all the things the client says and does and how they are behaving, without giving a meaning to them, for the client.

For example, in the first session with James I noticed that he was sat huddled in his chair, staring down at his lap, with his arms wrapped tightly around his body. I could have interpreted this to mean that he was very closed off and defended and that he did not want to go any further. Instead, I just noticed out loud what I had observed, and wondered in a quietly accepting way if this showed something of how he was feeling. This seemed to be helpful to him in allowing him to be accepting of those feelings, rather than telling him he should not feel that way or behave differently. This seemed to be the point at which we began to have some kind of a relationship, to be in some form of psychological contact, in which I felt very present and not just an observer.

Learning to love oneself

Another important truth that was present in my work with James and clients like him, is my belief in the importance, for all of us, of claiming the right to say how we feel and to insist on being heard and understood. As a person-centred counsellor, I want my clients to experience what it feels like to have their feelings fully heard and understood in an accepting way, so that they can learn to do that for themselves. Perhaps in experiencing tough love from me, they may begin to be able to give that same tough love to themselves and to demand the right to have their feelings heard by others.

Congruence, authenticity and the ethical principle of self-respect: dangers for the counsellor

It seems to me that there is something of a misunderstanding of the person-centred approach. It is often talked about as though it is undemanding and not particularly challenging. It often gets stereotyped as rather woolly and just about being warm and nice! It also seems to be inferred that it can be used as a basis for the other approaches rather than being of real value in its own right. In my experience, it is very far removed from these views and, properly practised, is an extremely rigorous and challenging form of therapy. Working in this demanding, intimate way with clients can draw very strongly on the counsellor's personal, emotional, psychological and physical resources. Working intensively with a number of clients with a wide range of serious presenting issues and concerns can have a damaging effect upon the counsellor and upon the personal relationships the counsellor may have. Work of this nature is immensely satisfying and can lead to the counsellor feeling that they cannot stop or take a break. Because of the level of satisfaction that the counsellor may get from this work, the counsellor may not realise the effect it is having upon them or upon their relationships with family, partners and friends. It is very easy for the counsellor to become burnt out or over-burdened through doing intensive work of this nature. Through being so closely present with their clients' feelings, it can make it very easy for the counsellor to over-identify with their clients and to take on their clients' feelings as though they were the counsellor's. It can become difficult for the counsellor to switch off or to distance themselves from their client work. It is clearly important that counsellors find ways of monitoring and maintaining their emotional, psychological and physical health, through support from others who are close to them. For counsellors working in this way, there is an ethical requirement to protect and care for themselves by ensuring that they have sufficient and adequate supervision, as well as being prepared to enter counselling for themselves. After all, we take the trouble to have our cars checked out and serviced on a regular basis. I would suggest that we owe ourselves the same duty of care?

In order to develop the level of self-awareness that is required in a counsellor, it is important for the counsellor to take care of themselves. The need for this is clearly described in the British Association for Counselling and Psychotherapy's *Ethical Framework* (BACP, 2010: 4). This describes the principle of 'self-respect' as fostering the practitioner's self-knowledge and self-care. The intimate nature of working in an intimate emotional relation with a client plainly offers the potential for the counsellor either to get burned out by the intensity of the work or to become desensitised by it. The *Ethical Framework* states that the principle of self-respect encourages active engagement in life-enhancing activities and relationships that are independent of relationships in counselling or psychotherapy. It seems to me that the wise counsellor will aim at having a life full of many kinds of meaning rather than a life full of counselling!

Broader applications of the approach – beyond the counselling arena

Dr C.H. Patterson wrote: 'In his writing Rogers uses two terms: *client-centered therapy* and the *person-centered approach*. In an article titled "Client-centered? Person-centered?" (Rogers, 1987), Rogers states he would like "a term to describe what I do when I am endeavouring to be facilitative in a group of persons who are not my clients." That term is *person-centered*. *Client-centered* is the term used with clients, in therapy. Great!' (Patterson and Watkins, 1996: 15). Because of the central tenet that the person-centred approach is about a way of being, this means that it is applicable across a wide variety of contexts. It is perhaps more accurate to describe the work in counselling as being 'client-centred' and to describe the wider application of the way of being as the person-centred approach. This makes a great deal of sense to me.

When I am working as a counsellor with a client, I am being as client-centred as I can be with the presence of those six necessary and sufficient conditions. In the wider world, I am practising my commitment to the person-centred approach as a way of being in the world outside the counselling room. In those very different contexts, not all of those six conditions can be present. However, it is my belief that those three central conditions can and should be present in all aspects of my life and in all areas of my work. For myself, I have found the principles and practice of being person-centred extremely valuable in my family life, my personal relationships, in my teaching at university, and in my work in management consultancy. I believe that the person-centred approach has applications across a variety of other relational contexts, including: the family, education, community work, social work, medicine, nursing, management development, coaching and mentoring, etc. The following examples of the broader application may serve to illuminate this.

Education

Rogers himself wrote about the importance of developing the person-centred approach in education (Rogers and Freiberg, 1994) and promoted a revolutionary approach to the way we run our schools and teach our children. He suggested ways of implementing a person-centred approach that would transform the ways that schools, school administrators and teachers work, to aid the development of the minds of children and young persons, and to encourage adventurous enterprises being carried out by dedicated, caring teachers in creative classrooms and supportive schools. Rogers believed that in education the focus should not be on 'teaching', but rather it should be on the facilitation of learning through developing the right attitudinal qualities in the relationship between the teacher and the learner. He went on to describe the same three conditions, which are so important in the counselling relationship, as being essential to the classroom relationship as well.

Rogers first described these qualities or attitudes that facilitate learning in a journal article in 1967, which was later reproduced in his book on education, *Freedom to Learn* (Rogers and Freiberg, 1994: 151–8):

Realness in the facilitator of learning

Perhaps the most basic of these essential attitudes is realness or genuineness. When the facilitator is a real person, being what she is, entering into a relationship with the learner without presenting a front or a façade, she is much more likely to be effective. This means that the feelings that she is experiencing are available to her, available to her awareness, that she is able to live these feelings, be them, and able to communicate if appropriate. It means coming into a direct personal encounter with the learner, meeting her on a person-to-person basis. It means that she is being herself, not denying herself. (Rogers and Freiberg, 1994: 154)

Prizing, acceptance, trust

There is another attitude that stands out in those who are successful in facilitating learning. … I think of it as prizing the learner, prizing her feelings, her opinions, her person. It is a caring for the learner, but a non-possessive caring. It is an acceptance of this other individual as a separate person, having worth in her own right. It is a basic trust – a belief that this other person is somehow fundamentally trustworthy. … What we are describing is a prizing of the learner as an imperfect human being with many feelings, many potentialities. The facilitator's prizing or acceptance of the learner is an operational expression of her essential confidence and trust in the capacity of the human organism.

Empathic understanding

A further element that establishes a climate for self-initiated experiential learning is emphatic understanding. When the teacher has the ability to understand the student's reactions from the inside, has a sensitive awareness of the way the process of education and learning seems to the student, then again the likelihood of significant learning is increased. … Students feel deeply appreciative when they are simply understood – not evaluated, not judged, simply understood from their own point of view, not the teacher's. (Rogers, 1967: 304–11)

My own experience of working in this way as a counsellor educator has proved immensely challenging both for students, tutors and for the university; at the same time it has also been richly rewarding for us all.

Consultancy work

In my work as a consultant specialising in helping organisations to manage change, my person-centred way of being has been of enormous importance. I have always seen my role as a consultant as '*Helping others to help themselves*', which is the unique selling point or 'strap line' on my consultancy company's advertising material. Working very often in severely conflicted organisations, I have developed an approach based on developing a close working relationship with my organisational clients, based on the three central conditions. In my work, I set out to be very phenomenological about what I see, hear and experience happening in an organisation and place that firmly alongside trying to get a clear and accurate understanding of how all the people working in an organisation see, hear and experience their organisation. I have learned the importance of being internally congruent and appropriately transparent, and the importance of encouraging everyone in the organisation to take the risk of doing that too. Perhaps the following brief example may show a little of the flavour of that work.

The engineering firm

I had been contracted to work with the senior management team of a medium-sized engineering company which was having difficulty recruiting and retaining staff and had a number of senior managers suffering from burn-out. An enlightened new Chief Executive had decided that they needed to change the culture of the company and, in his language, 'humanise it'. My role was to facilitate the process of culture change. As usual, I began by meeting staff from all levels in the organisation to try to get a sense of how they experienced the culture of the organisation, what they liked and what they wanted to be different. I also sat in on a number of different meetings to do a 'fly on the wall' observation of how people worked together and how they treated each other. I then produced a brief report to the Chief Executive on what I had perceived and some ideas for starting a change management process. He invited me to attend the next meeting of the senior management team to present my report to them.

I arrived for the meeting, just before it was due to start. Fred, who was the Director of Project Management and an almost stereotypical, blunt, no-nonsense engineer, looked over his coffee cup and chortled, 'Ah, here's our "touchy feely man", going to tell us what we are doing wrong!'

Looking him straight in the eyes I responded very acceptingly and immediately with, 'You sound really threatened by me Fred – and I'm not surprised. I guess you might be a bit nervous of what I'm going to report and I understand that. I need to tell you that I feel really insulted by you putting me down in that way. I don't think you've got the bottle to do what I do and work with people's feelings. They are very different to bits of machinery; you can't shape them with a lathe or batten them down with a spanner. To do my kind of work you have to have the ability to be very sensitive and at the same time very tough and resilient.'

There was a rather embarrassed silence for a moment or two when it was clear that he was quite thrown by my response and did not know how to reply. The Chief Executive then walked in so we all sat down and the meeting began. I presented my report and found myself being listened to in a very respectful way and the whole team, engaged in a very open discussion of my findings and suggestions.

At the end of the meeting Fred came across to me holding out his hand to be shaken. He said, 'When I came in here, there was no way I was going to listen to what some soft psychologist was going to tell me about how I should run our company. Then I found out you aren't soft after all! I was really surprised that you understood how I felt, even though I didn't know it myself – and even more surprised at how you were so open about how you felt. I think you have got a lot of bottle! I don't necessarily agree with everything you said in your report, but I am prepared to work with you to try to make change happen.'

Over the next four years I met regularly with Fred as he took one of the lead roles in the change process. As a consequence, I experienced real change in the way the company worked and real change in Fred too. Being empathically accepting followed quickly by being congruent and really transparent in the moment had been quite a risk, but being intuitive and spontaneous had really paid off. I think I might have gone on for a long time battling with the label of being a 'touchy feely man' and not much change would have happened.

Supervision

Another area in which it seems to me the broader application of the person-centred approach is relevant is that of supervision. There is an ethical requirement for counsellors in the UK to monitor their practice by undertaking supervision with an experienced practitioner, who can help them to reflect on their work and all the things that impact on that work. The purpose of this is to ensure that the quality of the counsellor's work is maintained and the therapist is supported and contained in what they do. All the principles of the person-centred approach translate very readily to supervision. The supervisor needs to maintain a non-expert, non-directive stance, providing a relationship in which the three central conditions can be experienced by the counsellor. Supervision needs to be supportive and accepting of the counsellor and at the same time needs to incorporate challenge and tough love. Rather like counselling, supervision that is not both accepting and challenging is not really supervision.

Rogers was also quite clear that he was not suggesting a passive listening process in counselling and I believe the same to be true in supervision. For me, supervision needs to be an active relationship, really focused on gaining as accurate an understanding of just how a supervisee is experiencing their feelings, their understanding of their reality, in the moment in working with their clients; and communicating that understanding to the supervisee in an accepting and non-judgemental manner. This makes it essential that the supervisor completely avoids an 'active-directive stance', unless issues of counsellor, client or other people's safety create an ethical imperative for the supervisor to intervene in a more directive manner.

In my supervision of other counsellors, this has led to some interesting conversations, such as the one with Maureen which I will now describe.

Maureen was a 30-year-old mother of two young children who had completed her training as a person-centred counsellor some two years previously. Since then she had been employed as a counsellor in an agency which ran a counselling service for women in abusive relationships. Maureen had been coming to me for supervision for about 18 months and it felt as though we had a good working relationship. As usual, Maureen had sent me in advance some brief notes of the issues she wanted to focus on in our next session. One of her notes said, 'I would really like to talk about what I need to do to help Client J to move on.'

Once our supervision session had got going and she reached this particular point, I asked her to tell me a little more. So she began:

Maureen:	I've seen her for eleven sessions now and I'm really stuck. She seems to be going round and round the same story, every session. She shows no sign of being able to progress and I'm feeling really frustrated. I'm wondering if I should go on seeing her as I don't seem to be doing anything to help.
Roger:	So, you're feeling really frustrated, feeling stuck and I'm wondering if you are also feeling sort of inadequate and de-skilled and just don't know what to do?
Maureen:	Mm, that's it, I really feel like I've lost my way.
Roger:	Mmm, I'm wondering what you think your way is and whether you're thinking there is somewhere you and J should be going?
Maureen:	Well yes, her life seems really difficult and full of pain and there do seem to be so many things she could be doing and, if I'm honest, some things I think she should be doing.
Roger:	It sounds to me like you feel really compassionate towards her, that you really care and want to help her to reduce the pain and hurt she is experiencing. I wonder if that is getting in the way a bit?

Maureen: [A long silence]

Roger: Well, the way I see it is that you are on a journey with J. It's her journey and only she can decide where and when she is going and what she is or isn't going to do. My sense is that she is stuck, not you. You are not supposed to be going anywhere, so how can you be stuck. Your job is to be with your client, staying close beside her, perhaps just a little bit behind, so that she is always in the lead. So, if she is stuck, it seems pretty important that you stay with her in that stuck place and help her to explore that experience and get a real sense of how it is for her.

Maureen: Mmm, I think that's going to be quite hard for me to do.

Roger: Yes, I can see that. It feels quite risky for you. I'm wondering what it would be like for you to be transparent with your feelings of concern and frustration, with her, owning them as yours and at the same time being really accepting of her in her stuckness and finding your way of communicating that. Maybe if she really feels understood and accepted in her stuckness by you, she might then choose to move on when she is ready to.

Maureen: You're back to being those three central conditions again, aren't you? I don't really need to 'do' anything do I? I just need to be a bit different. I really need to just be beside her and stop trying to get in front and rescue her.

Roger: Uh huh. And I'm also saying something I strongly believe, which is that if I get a feeling when working with a client, I want to err on the side of expressing that feeling in an appropriate way. If I want my client to be really in touch and open with their feelings, it's really important that I am that way too, and that I don't hide or sit on my feelings in that relationship. I kind of hope that is how you have experienced me here?

With slight variations, this is more or less the same conversation I've had with many supervisees and trainees over the years. For me, it is another expression of my focus on my way of being with supervisees, rather than trying to do things. It also shows the importance of not being just a passive listener, but of actively engaging with a supervisee in the communication of empathy and acceptance.

A link to the next chapter

In the next chapter, I will describe Rogers' seven stages of process in the counselling relationship, considering some of the ways in which a person-centred counsellor might work through these stages with a client. I will also look briefly at some of the difficulties involved in working with clients who are unable to engage in depth in therapy as a result of mental health issues, psychological disorders, medication and substance misuse. Not everyone is suited to be a person-centred counsellor or feels comfortable with training to be one, and the chapter will end by reflecting on the kind of person you need to be, and the sorts of personal attributes you need to develop, in order to become a person-centred counsellor.

Recommended reading

Rogers, Carl (1980) 'Empathic: an unappreciated way of being', in *A Way of Being*. New York: Houghton Mifflin, Chapter 7.

Haugh, Sheila and Merry, Tony (eds) (2001) *Empathy*. In the Rogers' Therapeutic Conditions: Evolution, Theory and Practice Series, edited by Gill Wyatt. Ross-on-Wye: PCCS Books.

Casemore, R. (2009) 'It is all in the relationship: exploring the differences between supervision training and counsellor training', in P. Henderson (ed.), *Supervisor Training*. London: Karnac Books.

Tudor, L.E., Keemar, K., Tudor, K., Valentine, J. and Worrall, M. (2004) *The Person-centred Approach: a Contemporary Introduction*. Basingstoke: Palgrave Macmillan.

FIVE

The Process of Personality Change in Counselling and in Life

In this chapter, I will begin with a brief description of a not unusual example of an inauthentic client and his struggle to become more real. I will briefly explore how it may be possible to work with clients who are unable to engage in psychological contact. Then I will explore my understanding of the seven stages of becoming fully functioning, using an example from my client work to illustrate this. I will finish by suggesting some of the characteristics and attributes I believe need to be developed as an integrated way of being, in order to be effective as a person-centred counsellor.

Personality change and the fully functioning person

As we have seen, Carl Rogers thought that the ideal state for any individual was to be in a state of becoming. He suggested that to be rigid or stuck in our ideas about who and how each of us should be, is really quite unhealthy.

He saw therapy as 'a process of stages by which the individual, experiencing being received by the counsellor, changes over a period of time, from a static, unfeeling, fixed, impersonal type of functioning, to a more "in-motion" position, which is marked by a fluid, changing, acceptant experiencing of differentiated personal feelings' (Rogers, 1961: 132–58).

Rogers also suggested that underneath all the many and varied concerns that his clients brought to therapy, each client seemed to be trying to find out who they really were and what was the meaning and purpose of their life.

A significant difference between Rogers' view of self-actualisation and Maslow's, was that Rogers saw self-actualising as a continuing drive to become more fully functioning as a human being, able to cope more effectively, while becoming more and more complicated as an individual in a world that is becoming more and more complicated. Maslow, however, saw self-actualisation as a state that could be achieved. I feel that Maslow's 'Hierarchy of Human Needs' (Maslow, 1943), which is usually illustrated with a closed triangle, should be open at the top to demonstrate Rogers' belief in our continuing potential throughout life.

A shared state of inauthenticity

People often have real difficulty in being able to naturally be who they really are. Time and again I have heard clients describe themselves as 'wearing a mask', 'playing a role in the play of my life', 'always coping on the outside and very different inside'. This indicates that they lock away the feeling part of themselves, because it is too dangerous for it to be free. They seem to have learned that if they show their true feelings they will be punished by those around them, and so they punish themselves in anticipation. They unconsciously commit themselves to a life of in-authenticity which they share with others around them. This leads to a general state of social collusion in being inauthentic. As a counsellor, I need to understand and communicate my acceptance of my client's in-authenticity and, by being authentic in myself in the relationship with them, challenge them to choose to be different.

Becoming aware of being inauthentic

Only recently a young man, called Tony, came to see me. He seemed to be representative of a number of clients that I have worked with over the years. He described how he had been brought up in a very abusive, dysfunctional family setting and that he had been abandoned by his mother at an early age. He had constantly witnessed terrible violence from his alcoholic father towards his step-mother and towards himself and his brothers and sisters. He described his home as a battle zone where the war never ended and he was always fearful for his mother and his siblings, and saw himself as responsible for their safety. When he was 16 his father became more violent towards him and, fearful of the possible consequences, he left home and school and moved away to another town. Over the next few years he worked hard to overcome that dreadful start in life.

Now in his early thirties, he described himself as great at coping. He considered himself to be really strong and would never think of letting anyone see any sign of weakness in him. He had learned at a very early age that he should never show his feelings or he would be beaten. If he cried after being beaten, he would be beaten again for crying. Most of all he had learned that he had to be really independent, never to rely on anyone else and to be really good at everything he did. Failure was not allowed. Tony's whole life was built on those concepts and I experienced him as being very driven by them.

Some time ago Tony had been really shocked by getting a stomach ulcer and experiencing dreadful pain. For months he had hidden this from everyone, until he collapsed and was hospitalised. One day in hospital, he had been in so much pain that he could not stop himself from crying and had been greatly embarrassed when a young nurse saw him sobbing with the pain and frustration. He quickly stopped himself and said to the nurse who came to comfort him: 'There's no need for that, I'm not supposed to cry – it's not allowed'. The nurse replied astutely: 'Maybe it's your ulcer that is crying, because it hurts so much. Maybe you could take your ulcer to see a counsellor, because you're allowed to cry there.' Tony just brushed that off with a typical for him, 'No, I'll be fine.'

Medication helped to relieve his pain and to reduce the symptoms of the ulcer, but it regularly flared up again and again. Eventually, Tony plucked up the courage to try to find a counsellor and after many months he contacted me and asked for an appointment. When he first arrived, he told me that he did not really know why he was there, that he did not really want to come and talk about his problems. He just wanted to get back to coping again like he did before. I worked hard over many months to establish an accepting relationship with him, gradually enabling him to bring all of the hurt that he had and was still experiencing. This took him a long time as he was so used to presenting as the one who copes with everything.

Over that period of time Tony gradually became able to discover a part of himself that he had always denied, a part of himself that was really unknown to him. This was the part of him that felt really lonely and unhappy, very unloved and very scared of being punished and abandoned. This part of him was hidden behind his 'coping self', which was always presenting with the capacity to achieve and to be really good at anything he set out to do and drove him to work, work and work. Throughout our time together I felt it was really important for me to be authentic with him; to show the feelings I experienced as he told me his story. When eventually he let himself cry, I allowed my sadness and my tears to show as well, clearly modelling that it was really OK for a man to show his pain.

Towards the end of our time together, Tony said, 'I had it all wrong about being strong, didn't I? I never realised how strong you have to be to really be open with your feelings. Before, I thought it was weak to cry, strong to hide my feelings, but I was really being like a robot, wasn't I?' It was intriguing to see how, as he became more able to value his feelings and to experience the expressing of them, that at the same time his ulcer began to heal and he began to take better care of himself in other ways. Tony really began to function much more fully as a human being, as a person rather than as a robot, as someone who could cope and who could also choose to show his pain and not see it as a sign of not coping.

In the absence of psychological contact

In Chapter 3, I mentioned the importance and the difficulty of establishing and maintaining psychological contact. In the example above, it took me several months to be able to establish any real psychological contact with Tony. At first I was able to achieve this only fleetingly for short periods of time. Tony, like all of my clients, had come with a desire to be different and at the same time, within him, there was a very natural resistance to change. Then slowly as we travelled along the continuum of the stages of the therapeutic process, psychological contact began to occur more frequently and with more depth.

Schön (1971) suggests that homeostasis, the desire to remain the same, is the natural state of any organism, both biologically and psychologically. He describes resistance to change as an active process which goes on in individuals and in organisations, and one which the individual who is setting out to facilitate change needs to engage with fully. For me, in setting out to facilitate change in my clients, I want to begin by acknowledging and communicating my acceptance of their resistance as a choice which it is legitimate for them to make. At the same time, I want to be appropriately transparent with my feelings in the moment, as I experience their resistance and encourage them to think about how they might choose to not resist.

Rogers wrote very little about the concept of psychological contact other than his belief that it was the counsellor's authenticity which was most likely to enable it to occur. Gary Prouty (1994) is probably the only writer who has set out to define psychological contact and what it takes to establish and maintain it. In his work with clients with serious psychological disorders, he developed the concept of 'pre-therapy' as a means of working with clients who, for whatever reason, were unable to engage in psychological contact with the counsellor. He suggested that in order for the client to be able to engage in psychological contact with the counsellor, three forms of contact need to be present in both client and counsellor – 'Reality Contact, Affective Contact and Communicative Contact'. In simple language, first, the client needs to be able to be in contact with their real world. They need to be what might be described as 'with' their world, rather than just 'in' their world, like an alienated object. Secondly, they need to be in contact with their affective self, their moods, feelings and emotions. Thirdly, they need to be able to communicate their experiencing of those two forms of contact to the counsellor and be able to be with the counsellor's affective experiencing of that, in the therapeutic moment. In meeting a client for the first time, it seems to me to be very useful to bear Prouty's ideas in mind, in setting out to assess whether my client will be accessible for counselling. If not, I will need to consider whether to refer them on to another service or to consider if I can provide them with a supportive, therapeutic relationship which might enable us to work towards eventually establishing psychological contact.

The seven stages of the process of becoming fully functioning

The process which I described happening with Tony above, really reflected his progress through the process of becoming more fully functioning. It shows how he moved from a stage of being very fixed and rigid, to a stage of being able to be much more flexible, more creative and much more able to respond to how he experienced his life, in a more flowing way. This process of moving towards becoming more fully functioning can be described as a journey through the counselling relationship. In particular, it is important to encourage student or trainee counsellors not to see this journey as a series of discrete, fixed stages which they and their clients are obliged to pass through in their counselling practice. This is not a skills model of counselling but rather an explanation of counselling as a set of values and a way of life. Rogers certainly did not see this process as in any way rigid, but as points on a fluid continuum. My experience has been that progression along this continuum will be different for each client. What follows is a description of how I have experienced this process as it has generally worked for me.

The first stage

In the first stage of the process, clients can often seem very defensive and quite resistant to change. Often they will be quite anxious about coming to counselling, feeling in themselves that they need to and yet, at the same time, feeling that they do not want to, that it cannot possibly help. Often in this first stage, they do not seem able to talk much about themselves and their feelings, wanting instead to talk mainly about their problem, the difficulties facing them or the things or other people that are problematic in their life. In the beginning, clients can talk almost non-stop, telling their story, without actually saying much about their feelings at all. I have often experienced clients telling me about the difficulties in their world outside the counselling room, almost as though these things were happening to someone else. They do this in quite a rigid way that seems almost as though it has been designed to keep me (and them) away from any exploration of their feelings.

Responding in the first stage

Trainee and beginning counsellors can find this stage very interesting and can become very intent on listening to the story and trying to understand it. At this time, they can fall into the trap of merely reflecting back the words of the story and failing to hear the depth and range of feelings that are hidden behind the words. At this stage, it can sometimes be very difficult to hear the music behind the words. Also, as human beings, we have a drive to understand and it is therefore very natural and important to pay attention to the content of the story in this early stage of the relationship. If the client resists talking about their feelings and continues to focus on their story, about events external to the counselling room, and the counsellor continues to focus on this, it is no wonder that the client will keep on doing it. The consequence is that it will not be long before the counsellor and the client begin to feel stuck and the counsellor is also likely to start to feel very frustrated and to doubt their own competence.

Stuck in the first stage

In my supervision of counsellors, stuckness in the early stages of the relationship is a common theme. I often hear supervisees describe how a client keeps on going over and over their story and seems to be very stuck, and how the counsellor feels very frustrated with not being able to move the client on. I usually respond by saying, 'I wonder where you think you should be going, where you think your client should be moving on to? Your job is to stay with your client, to follow them and not to take the lead. You need to make it safe enough for your client to be in touch with their painful feelings and for you to be there with them, knowing that you really do understand.' Next I usually ask, 'I wonder what it is you are not hearing? I wonder what feelings your client may be experiencing as they are telling you their story? I wonder if you can listen and try to hear the music behind the words and communicate the feelings you experience back to your client, in a tentative way, to enable them to feel heard and understood?' Time after time, when supervisees have gone back to their client and worked harder at hearing the client's buried feelings and checking out their understanding of those feelings with the client, mysteriously (some might even say magically) the client seems to choose to move on by themselves. In recent times, I have begun to describe this as the use of 'evocative empathy'. Somehow, by being accurately empathic in a gentle tentative manner, this enables my client to access other deeper feelings, that they may often not have been aware of. It is almost as though my empathy evokes deeper feelings in the client.

Progression from the first stage

The client's progression from the first stage of the process is only likely to come about when clients begin to feel received, to experience the full acceptance of the counsellor and get a real sense that their feelings are thoroughly understood by the counsellor. Then, somehow, they begin to more easily experience and explore their full range of feelings.

The second stage

Remembering that these stages are not fixed or rigid, or even particularly clearly defined, it is clear that when the client begins to feel received, then the ways in which they have tended to express themselves in the earlier stages of counselling seem to change, often almost imperceptibly at first. Somehow, the client begins to talk about things other than the details of their story or the things that happen to them or are problematic. It is as though there is a slight easing of how the client is being in the relationship with the counsellor. With Tony, whom I have described above, I sensed this happening when he began to identify why his father might have become an alcoholic and recognised that his father might have been very frustrated and unable to cope. At the same time, Tony began to identify the tyranny of his father as the real reason for him, Tony, being so driven to succeed. He really seemed to be saying that it was not his fault that he was like he was. He could not take any responsibility for that at all; it was all his father's fault. At that point I tried to be just very accepting of how Tony was feeling and to communicate that to him.

Responding in the second stage

Remembering that the six core conditions are both necessary and sufficient for therapeutic change to take place, it is important for the counsellor to focus on the communication of the three central conditions and to enable the client to continue to experience being fully received. The counsellor needs to continue to try to be really in touch with the feelings the client is experiencing and to communicate this, rather than just reflecting back the details of the story he is telling.

Stuck in the second stage

Tony began to tell me why he thought his father had become an alcoholic and so violent. He followed this by saying that it was his father's fault that he, Tony, had become so driven. I responded with, 'It feels to me like life has been really unfair to you. I feel really sad about all the bad things that happened to you in your childhood. It sounds to me like you were determined to make the best of yourself, despite the way he treated you and yet you seem to feel that somehow it is still all his fault that you are driven like you are. I'm wondering if what you are feeling right now is that, despite your best efforts, he is still having a big impact on how you are and how you live your life.' As I responded in similar ways to a number of the things that Tony spoke about at this stage, he began to talk more about his feelings, but really still only describing them, rather than actually experiencing them in the counselling room, and he continued to do this for a number of sessions.

Progression from the second stage

Tony talked more about some of his rigid beliefs about how he should always be strong, knowledgeable and effective, but at the same time he slowly began to recognise that there were times when he just could not be those things. He even said to me, 'I really want to be different, not so driven – but I just don't know how to do it.' I responded acceptingly by saying, 'I get a sense that you are feeling really frustrated, really unhappy with being as you are and wanting to be different, some of the time. I'm wondering if you feel that there must be something that you could do – and then you would be different? I'm wondering if you are feeling like you really want to crack this and start being different but it's like your hands and feet are tied and you can't get moving?'

I continued by being transparent with my feelings in the moment and said, 'I feel pretty frustrated too, that I can't tell you how to do that.' After a pause in which he sat looking at me in a reflective way he said, 'So you're not holding out on me, then. I've really got to work this out for myself. I've got to look inside me for the answers.' He sat there, quietly looking into space and seemed really in touch with his feelings at that moment. The experience of being genuinely, acceptingly and empathically received, seemed to enable him to open up even more to experiencing himself and his feelings in that moment.

The third stage

At this point Tony began to move into the third stage of the process and began to talk in more depth about the things he had experienced in the past and how he had behaved in response to them. Tony did this in a rather impersonal way, as though he was describing himself as some kind of object rather than as a human being.

Responding in the third stage

For the first time, Tony began to be in touch with and to talk about some of the feelings he had denied to his experiencing in the past and which he was ashamed of feeling now. He talked about his anger towards his mother, of despising her and hating his father, and saying that he had always believed it was not right for him to feel that way towards his parents, no matter what they had done to him. He also talked about hiding those feelings even from himself, so that his parents would never suspect how he felt towards them. This is a clear example of how clients become more able to talk about themselves and their experiencing of their lives and seem to be rather stuck in the past and avoiding talking about the present. In that third stage, Tony experienced being fully accepted by me and his feelings really being understood, and that he was not in any way being judged for having those feelings about his parents. I encouraged him to see that he had a choice about how he dealt with these feelings towards his parent and their treatment of him as a child. He could choose to do as he has always done and not allow himself to feel any anger towards them because they were his parents and he had a duty to respect them. I wanted to be very accepting of the choice he had been making to bury his feelings. On the other hand, I wanted to challenge him to recognise that he could choose to feel angry and resentful because no child should have experienced the treatment that had been meted out to him. He could choose to recognise that it was perfectly normal and natural to be angry and resentful towards them.

Stuck in the third stage

I remember Tony saying, 'A son shouldn't feel those things about his parents', and me replying, 'It sounds like you feel really guilty for having those feelings about your mum and dad. Yet it seems pretty natural to me to hate and despise and lose your love for someone who has treated you so badly. I guess these are not very nice feelings for you to have and at the same time I do believe it is understandable to have them.' Tony found this really hard to believe. He became quite angry with me, punctuating his conversation with all the 'shoulds' and 'oughts' he had been taught to believe he must be in relating to his parents, despite all they had done to him.

Progression from the third stage

Tony seemed to stay stuck in this part of the process for quite a long time until one day he was talking about his relationship with his own daughter. He said, 'You know, I don't want her to love me just because I'm her dad. I want her to love me because she knows that I love her and she knows that she loves me. Not because it is a rule that you have to love your parents because they are your parents.' I looked at him with a gently quizzical expression on my face and said, 'I wonder what that says about your feelings for your dad?' Tony was silent for a while and then said, 'Yes, that's completely the opposite, isn't it? I keep on believing that I have to love my dad because there's a rule that says I have to.' He thought for a while and then said, 'But I suppose I've really got a choice about how I feel about my parents, haven't I?'

Rogers suggests that in the third stage of the process, the client will begin to identify and challenge some of the strongly held constructs or personal beliefs they hold about how they should be and will begin to identify how these are contradictory to their experience. As they do this, they will become more ready to move on to stage four of the process.

The fourth stage

Rogers suggested that when a client really feels understood, accepted and fully received at stage three, then the client will allow their feelings to flow much more freely and will begin to experience them much more in the counselling room rather than just talking about them. It is likely that this will still be a rather frightening thing for them and they may wish to resist it. They may be quite fearful and distrustful of this process and may experience counselling as being a very painful thing to be involved in.

Responding in the fourth stage

It is really important to let clients know that this fear and distrust of the process may happen. Counselling will not necessarily be a warm, cosy place, and at times it can be quite painful as clients come into contact with their full range of feelings. I always try to do this in my early contracting with a client and also to remind them from time to time that this may happen and that it is quite normal. As the client begins to move through stage four, they will become more able to be present with their feelings and to actually experience them in the present moment in the counselling room, although they are likely to be very unaccepting of their feelings at first. They are also quite likely to assume or be fearful that I will not be accepting of their feelings or that their feelings might damage me in some way.

Stuck in the fourth stage

Tony seemed to stay stuck in this stage or rather to drift backwards and forwards between stages three and four for quite some time. He frequently came close to being really angry and often seemed on the edge of tears. Every time he seemed to pull himself back. He began to be able to evaluate his experiences and to begin to identify new beliefs about himself which he could choose to hold now, rather than the ones his parents had taught him. At the same time, he found it really diffi-cult to let go of his feelings and just cry. When I said that this was how I was experiencing him, he replied, 'I really need to be in control of me and I'm scared that if I let go of my feelings, they will just take over and I'll be completely out of control.' I carefully checked out my under-standing of how that felt for him and then said, 'I'm wondering if you are also feeling that I won't be able to cope if you let your feelings out and become a bit uncontrolled?' He looked at me, quietly reflecting on what I had said, and then replied, 'That's not right, is it? I don't need to protect you from my feelings at all, do I?' I just looked back at him and smiled and nodded acceptingly.

Progression from the fourth stage

A little while after this he said, 'You know, I think it could be quite good to really cry and let go – and I don't think you will let me drown, will you?' To which I replied, 'No, it will be OK – and my tears may come as well.' He seemed mystified by the thought that I might cry and said, 'I don't want to make you cry.' I responded quite quickly with, 'Oh, you won't make me cry – it's just that when you are really close to your feelings of sadness, I feel much closer to my sad feelings too, and I'm OK about being in touch with these.' This seemed to be very releasing for him and we spent quite a bit of time talking about how it might be for him to experience his feelings there in the room with me and as he did that, he allowed some tears to just come to his eyes and I could really feel his sadness present in the room.

The fifth stage

In the fifth stage clients become more able to own their current emotions and begin to accept more responsibility for their actions and for being as they are. No longer is it all somebody else's fault.

Responding in the fifth stage

Slowly but surely Tony began to lower his defences and became more prepared to be in touch with his feelings and to allow them to be present in the room. He even began to cry occasionally, but only briefly, and would always stop himself from fully engaging with his tears. This included him discovering other feelings of which he had been unaware, particularly an intense feeling of loneliness and aloneness.

At first he found this hard to accept, knowing that he was in a good relationship in his marriage and had a lot of friends and colleagues who liked him. Slowly, he began to recognise that this huge paradox was true. That he was both surrounded by people who care for him and at the same time felt very alone.

Stuck in the fifth stage

Together, we explored what it might be like if he began to share more of his feelings with those who are close to him, rather than keeping them private to himself. He found this really difficult to consider and seemed really scared of allowing other people to see the real Tony. He was sure they would not accept or like him. I stayed with him as this took him to the hugely painful realisation that at the root of all this was the fact that he did not really accept or like himself, so how could anyone else. I stayed, very acceptingly with his buried feelings that deep down he was not acceptable to anyone, not even himself. He stayed in this painful place for a number of sessions, fighting to deny that he could be in any way acceptable. He said at one point, 'If I begin to believe that I am acceptable, it means that the whole of my life has been a lie!' I replied, tentatively, 'Or what you have been taught to believe about yourself is a lie? I'm also wondering if my full acceptance of you is quite threatening and that somehow you can't, or won't, allow yourself to fully experience my acceptance of you, like you somehow daren't really trust it or me?'

Progression from the fifth stage

At this point, Tony gave himself up to his feelings and cried freely, sobbing deeply. It seemed he had really moved towards stage six of the process, where he had let go of his feelings of stuckness and was really in touch with and expressing his feelings, right there in the moment. At that time, I felt really close to him and engaged in real relational depth. I felt hugely privileged to experience this and I told him so.

The sixth stage

Rogers suggests that this stage of the process is a crucial one, in which the client becomes really free to directly experience their feelings in the here and now of the counselling room. They learn that feelings are not to be feared and can be learned from and that all of their feelings need to be acknowledged and valued by them, in the way that the counsellor is valuing them.

Responding in the sixth stage

For several sessions Tony was able to be there with all his feelings. Often there were long silences, when he would sit with the tears trickling down his face. Sometimes he would become hugely angry; at other times he seemed really lost and alone. Mostly he talked about how he was feeling right there and then. He described how he was beginning to experience his feelings much more each day, at home and at work, and also how he was beginning to be able to say how he was feeling to the people in his life that mattered. He talked rarely about external events and seemed to have stopped referring back to the events of his childhood. I continued to try to be very present with him, really trying to get a clear understanding of how he was experiencing his feelings and himself, in a very different way. I gently fed back to him how I was experiencing him as being much more transparent, more real in his relationship with me. I also fed back that this was how I sensed he was beginning to experience himself in the world outside the counselling room as well.

Stuck in the sixth stage

Tony did not get at all stuck in this stage. In fact he was a good example of how Rogers describes it. He was really in the process of developing, moving and flowing. He said he felt much more free and able to let go of the restrictions of his past. There were, of course, times when he dipped back into stages four and five and even at one point went right back to what seemed like stage one of our relationship. However, we were both able to recognise when this was happening and by my being very accepting of those occurrences, he was able to keep on moving on his journey of change.

Progression from the sixth stage

At one point Tony said, 'This seems a strange thing to say, but I feel like I'm really beginning my life, now. Like I'm free to be whoever and whatever I want to be. That feels really scary and at the same time really exciting.' He had reached the point at which he no longer needed my help to give himself permission to be himself. Rogers suggests that clients who successfully progress to stage six will often seem to progress onwards without much need of the counsellor's help.

The seventh stage

Rogers suggests that this stage takes place as much outside the therapeutic relationship as within it. With Tony, as our relationship moved towards an ending, it was very clear that he was taking his newly learned ways of being and developing them in his life and relationships outside counselling. He was clearly so much more accepting of himself and of all his feelings and through this was becoming much more accepting of other people and their feelings. While still ambitious and keen to succeed, he no longer seemed to be totally driven by this. He clearly owned his feelings and no longer tried to blame other people for them, and seemed to be able to trust his own processes much more. Significantly, he identified that he had learned to judge each new experience as it happened, rather than measuring it against his past experiences as a child. He had even developed some new and fresh ideas about 'who' and 'how' he wanted to be, rather than continuing to be driven by those he had taken from his parents. He had really become much more fully functioning.

My way of being as a counsellor and as a person

Throughout my work with Tony, I had concentrated on being unconditional in my acceptance of him and his experiencing of himself and his
feelings. I had worked hard to get a continuing sense of how he experienced his feelings from his frame of reference and to communicate that
to him as tentatively as I could, so that I could check out that I was getting it right. I felt that I had been completely authentic and genuine
with him in how I experienced him and his concerns, and that I had
been appropriately transparent with my feelings in the counselling
relationship. At times I had been quite challenging in enabling him to
be in touch with his feelings and to stay with them, even though it was
really painful for him to do that. I had worked hard to be therapeutically
present in the room with him and to establish deep relational contact,
in which he could experience my tough love for him.

It is really important to remember that progressing through the
seven stages is rarely as clear cut and complete as I have described
above. Rogers himself suggested that such a journey might sometimes
take several years. While I believe that to be true with clients who have
very significant or deeply rooted disturbances, I also believe that the
journey can be achieved in a few months, if the client is really willing
to change and the counsellor is able to be fully present in the relationship and has faith in the sufficiency of the necessary and sufficient
conditions for therapeutic change.

A way of being, not just a way of counselling

My work with Tony, as with my work with most of my clients, was a
hugely demanding, exhausting process. Furthermore, like most counsellors, I usually have more than one client in my case load. To work at
this level with a number of clients really requires me to take good care
of myself, both physically and emotionally. I also need to be person-
centred in all aspects of my life. Those three central conditions of

unconditional acceptance, empathy and authenticity are not techniques to be turned on in the counselling room. They need to be an integral part of my personality – what I am, rather than what I do. It is also essential that I develop the capacity to experience those three central conditions within myself, from myself. If I can't be those three conditions with myself, how can I really be them with someone else?

Not everyone will feel the person-centred approach is right for them, and neither should they. Not everyone will be suited to train or practise as a person-centred counsellor. Neither is there one way of being person-centred. Each of us has to find a way that fits for us. Each of us has to find a way of developing the characteristics and attitudes that a person-centred counsellor needs to have and avoid trying to develop them as a set of techniques or methods.

So, what kind of characteristics do you need to develop in yourself, in order to live and work in the ways that Carl Rogers suggested, in a way that fits for you? This is not a prescriptive account of the characteristics required, but merely suggestions of what you need to have in at least some degree in order to develop your own person-centred approach to counselling and to life.

The characteristics

If, as an individual, you have a tendency to:

- believe that people are basically good and will always try to do the best for themselves,
- experience your world through your feelings and your experiences, rather than analysing everything or looking for solutions or meanings,
- believe that your feelings are as important as anybody else's,
- be very accepting of other people and of yourself,

then the person-centred approach might be right for you.

If you have the capacity to:

- notice and observe people and things without rushing to interpret them,
- be in touch with your own feelings and be internally congruent with them,

- be appropriately transparent with your feelings as you experience them and believe you have the right to say how you feel,
- be with other people in their most painful moments without trying to rescue them or make them feel better,

then the person-centred approach might be right for you.

Most of all, if you have the capacity to be all of these things to some degree in all aspects of your life, then the person-centred approach might be the right approach for you and the clients with whom you work.

A link to the next chapter

In this next chapter, I will explore the person-centred concept of 'presence' in the counselling relationship, which Rogers developed later in his life, and some ways in which this characteristic can be developed. I will show how demanding this can be for both counsellor and client in both short-term and long-term work, and how important it is for counsellors to take care of themselves. I will identify some ethical issues arising from working at relational depth with clients, and will include something on the importance of being culturally competent. I will look briefly at the person-centred approach as a living, growing theory and practice, and also briefly consider the importance that Rogers placed in trusting in your intuition.

Recommended reading

Barrett-Lennard, Godfrey T. (1998) *Carl Rogers' Helping System: Journey and Substance.* London: Sage.

Rogers, Carl (1980) *A Way of Being.* New York: Houghton Mifflin.

Rogers, Carl (1961) *On Becoming a Person: a Therapist's View of Psychotherapy.* London: Constable.

Wyatt, G. and Sanders, P. (eds) (2002) *Contact and Perception.* In the Rogers' Therapeutic Conditions: Evolution, Theory and Practice Series, edited by Gill Wyatt. Ross-on-Wye: PCCS Books.

SIX

The Relationship is the Therapy

In this chapter, I will explore the person-centred concept that the counsellor needs to be very 'present' with their whole self in the counselling relationship, engaging with the whole self of the client and describe an experience of working in this way with a resistant client. I will then identify some ethical issues which need to be considered in working in a person-centred way at relational depth with clients. This will also include a brief exploration of the importance of being culturally competent. I will briefly look at the person-centred approach as a living, growing, theory and practice, and also briefly consider the importance that Rogers placed in trusting in his intuition. This chapter and the book will end with a quotation from Carl Rogers, describing what, for him, at that time was a new venture in relating.

The essential nature of presence as a characteristic of the counsellor

In the later stages of his life, Carl Rogers further developed his view of the powerful, therapeutic nature of the relationship in which the counsellor is setting out to be with the client. In 1980 he wrote:

> When I am at my best, as a group facilitator or a therapist, I discover another characteristic. I find that when I am closest to my inner, intuitive self, when I am somehow in touch with the unknown in me, when perhaps I am in a slightly altered state of consciousness, then whatever

I do seems to be full of healing. Then simply my presence is releasing and helpful to the other. There is nothing I can do to force this experience, but when I can relax and be close to the transcendental core of me, then I may behave in strange and impulsive ways in the relationship, ways which I cannot justify rationally, which have nothing to do with my thought processes. But these strange behaviours turn out to be right, in some odd way; it seems that my inner spirit has reached out and touched the inner spirit of the other. Our relationship transcends itself and becomes a part of something larger. Profound growth and healing energy are present. (Rogers, 1980: 29)

An additional characteristic – therapeutic presence

Rogers had clearly begun to identify a further development of the person-centred approach, in which he used the term 'presence' to describe what he saw as an essential attribute of any counsellor – that was a powerfully healing element of the person-centred approach. He was unable to develop this concept further or to research or to study it in depth before he died.

Subsequent writers on the person-centred approach have taken different views about what Rogers meant in describing this characteristic. Brian Thorne (1992) suggested that presence might be seen as an additional condition, with a spiritual or mystical element, whereas Dave Mearns (1994) suggested that it might be a drawing together of the three central conditions of empathy, acceptance and congruence, in working at relational depth. I see 'presence' as an expression of all of the relevant parts of myself, in the counselling relationship and in all of my other relationships in my life.

Being present is different from therapeutic presence

It is clear that in using the term 'presence', Rogers was referring to a powerful characteristic of the counsellor and not just to the counsellor being present or there in the room in a purely physical sense. It is helpful to differentiate between being physically present in the room and what I will call 'therapeutic presence'.

Deep relational contact and presence

The idea of therapeutic presence builds further on the notion of psychological contact, as the first of the six necessary and sufficient conditions being an essential precondition for therapy to take place. Another way of describing psychological contact would be to call it 'deep relational contact' (Geller and Greenberg, 2002). This deep relational contact will not happen just because the counsellor is in a room with a client. The counsellor needs to take responsibility for establishing that deep relational contact by developing their therapeutic presence.

The different elements of therapeutic presence

So, what is therapeutic presence? Geller and Greenberg carried out a programme of research in 2001 to try to identify the quality of the counsellor's therapeutic presence in counselling. Their research confirmed two things. First, my capacity to be therapeutically present with my client does not just happen because I want it to. I have learned that I need to prepare myself to be present for each session with a client, or it will not happen. I am not just preparing to be in a room with someone. I am preparing to be in a therapeutic relationship with my client, which is likely to be pretty demanding for both of us. Secondly, it is important to live my life in such a way that it enables me to be a counsellor and to develop therapeutic presence as an integrated characteristic within myself in my daily life. That therapeutic presence is not a technique which I use on other people; it is an integrated part of me. I want to be experienced as a therapeutic individual, someone who enables change to take place.

Preparation for presence
before meeting

Being a counsellor is not a hobby; it is a serious professional endeavour and needs to be treated as such. Counsellors need to work very hard to develop the characteristic of therapeutic presence in themselves. Geller and Greenberg (2002) suggested that there are two categories of preparation that are essential. First, they suggested that preparation immediately before meeting a client is critically important. In Chapter 2, I described how important I feel it is just before I see a client to check out that I am being accepting, empathic and genuine, towards myself, how I am feeling in myself and how I am feeling about the work I am about to do. For me, this has meant developing a simple process which I use in the short time before each client arrives.

This is a process which I call 'Turning on and Tuning in', which helps me to be therapeutically present with and for my client. In the time before a client arrives, I visualise switching myself on, rather like turning on the radio or TV. I begin by checking out how I am actually feeling both emotionally and physically. Then I tune myself in by spending a few moments identifying my current concerns, feelings and issues which might get in the way of my paying attention to my client. Next I visualise wrapping these concerns up in brown paper and sticky tape and putting them away in a cupboard at the back of my mind. (I have a colleague who visualises downloading them on to a memory stick or a CD.) I know I cannot do anything about these issues, feelings and concerns right now, and certainly not during the next hour while I am with my client. They are going to need my attention later but for now, I am putting them somewhere safe while I give my full attention to my client. This might also be described as 'bracketing off' my concerns and clearing some space within me, so that I can be fully with my client. I also know that this is not just a simple, one-off process. Some of those thoughts and feelings that I wrapped up in brown paper and sticky tape will have a sneaky tendency to come out again during the session, so I need to watch out for them, making sure that they do not creep out and distract me while I am with the client.

Preparation for presence in everyday life

The second category of preparation that Geller and Greenberg (2002) identified is the importance of preparation in daily life. They were saying very clearly that counsellors need to develop the characteristic of presence as an integral part of themselves, in the same way that counsellors need to integrate in themselves the three central characteristics of unconditional acceptance, empathy and authenticity. This echoes what I have said above, about the importance of living my life in such a way that it enables me to be a counsellor. This means having a commitment to being a counsellor along with taking responsibility for ensuring my own continuing personal growth. This entails being prepared to be a client and to take my own concerns to a counsellor from time to time. It also means being prepared to take care of myself both emotionally and physically and to live as healthy a life as I can. It is important that my whole life is not bound up with counselling or helping others, and that I have other activities and interests. I need to ensure also that I have a range of caring, fulfilling relationships in my personal life, so that I am not dependent on my clients to meet my emotional needs. Within my personal relationships and in other aspects of my daily life, I do want to be experienced as therapeutically present, as having the capacity to enable change to take place, while at the same time making sure that I do not in any way become a counsellor to my friends or colleagues.

At those times when I have been really aware of working hard to develop and maintain my therapeutic presence in my life and in my counselling, I have experienced a very different quality in my work with my clients. I have also realised that when I work in this way, it is very demanding both physically and emotionally. This is another important reason for really making sure that I take care of myself and ensuring that being therapeutically present with my clients does not take too great a toll on me.

The whole self of the counsellor and the client

Another way of describing presence would be that it is a way for the counsellor to be there with the whole of the counsellor's authentic self, even though some of their concerns may be being bracketed off temporarily. In being therapeutically present with my client, I want to be able to enter into my client's experiencing of their reality, while at the same time remaining grounded in my own reality. If I can take the risk of being there with the whole of my self, then perhaps my client will take the risk of being fully there too, rather than only presenting parts of themselves. The following example from my work with a client will illustrate this.

An example of a client's experience of the counsellor's presence

I first met a client, whom I will call Linda, when she was referred to me because she was suffering from depression and having major difficulties in her relationships with her husband and her three sons. She was in her early fifties, and was smartly dressed in a dark blue business suit and carrying a very large Filofax, stuffed with papers. She told me that she had quite a senior position as an accountant and enjoyed her status and most of her work, and felt that she was good at her job. In her early sessions with me she spent most of her time talking about the difficulties she had in living with her husband and three sons and that she felt trapped in this relationship because there was no way she could contemplate leaving it. She believed her husband had never loved her and she knew that she had never really loved him. She had become pregnant by him when she was 16 and had responded to strong pressure from her parents to get married, even though she did not really want to. She felt that she had no choice except to marry him. Over the years he had never been affectionate with her and had often been quite abusive in demanding sexual relations with her. She really felt that she was much more of a servant or housekeeper for him, rather than a wife. Her three sons, who were now in their teens, had also become very demanding and quite cruel. They often bullied her and struck her physically and her husband gave her no support when this happened. She told me all of these things with almost no trace of feeling. It was as though she was reporting something which was happening to somebody else, rather than something she was experiencing.

So here I was, meeting someone who appeared to be a very well-organised accountant, who coped well with her job and was apparently well regarded by her colleagues and employers. At the same time she was talking about these abusive things that were being done to her, as though they were being done to someone else. Each time, when Linda left, I felt quite drained and at the same time also felt that I was missing something, or some part of her. For several months Linda turned up every week and each time I experienced her as 'reporting' to me the latest list of unpleasant things that her husband and/or her sons had done to her, each time without any kind of feeling attached to them, while I listened carefully and attentively to her.

Eventually, at the end of one of our sessions, I was able to say to her just how I was experiencing her in these sessions. I said that I felt I was working really hard to be here with the whole of my self and that I was feeling kind of puzzled that I was only experiencing her as partly there. I went on to say that I was OK with this and, at the same time, I wondered how it might be for her to bring the whole of herself to be there with me. I wondered out loud what it would be like for her to bring all her feelings into the room and to experience some of them, rather than just talking about them in a kind of reporting way. I said that I recognised that this could be quite difficult or even frightening for her, so I did not want to push her to do it. I just wanted her to know that she could choose to do that, if and when she felt it was alright. She left me at the end of that session, seeming rather quiet and thoughtful, and I felt that I had not really made contact with her.

We carried on in much the same way for the next two sessions and I continued to feel excluded from her feelings. In talking this through with my supervisor, it struck me that I needed to find a way of being much more present for her. I needed to do much more than listen to her, reporting her feelings and checking out my understanding of them. I began to suspect that perhaps I was colluding with her process of reporting, by keeping myself a little distant and just receiving what she was reporting to me rather than engaging with her. I realised that what I really needed to do was to find a way to be more present with my feelings. I needed to be more therapeutically present in order to engage with her feelings and to communicate how I was experiencing her.

Before the next session I really concentrated on how I could have more therapeutic presence with Linda, by being more in touch with my feelings as they were occurring in the session, and how I could communicate this to her more effectively by being appropriately transparent. In the next session, she began to talk about something she had not spoken of before. Slowly, she began to tell me that she was being treated quite badly by a senior manager at work and also being bullied by a couple of colleagues in her team.

This led into her describing how she had never had any affection from either of her parents. She told me how, whenever she did anything her parents did not like or thought was wrong, they would beat her and then not talk to her for weeks on end. She remembered, from about 7 years of age, being regularly 'sent to Coventry', as she put it, by both her parents, for almost two months on one occasion. This led her into talking about how she was always being bullied at school by a group of girls who always seemed to have it in for her.

Throughout most of this telling of her story, I continued to focus on listening carefully, occasionally checking out that I had understood what she had told me. I tried hard to get a sense of what she might be feeling as she was talking to me, but this seemed almost impossible to do. It was as though the feeling part of her was still being hidden away from me.

I gently fed back to her how I was experiencing her and the impact this was having on me, with the following words:

'Linda, I've listened carefully to you telling me about all the different ways in which you have been and still are being bullied and abused by other people. It feels to me like, for almost the whole of your life, other people have had it in for you in some way. They've either beaten you physically or hurt you emotionally. They have been withdrawing or withholding love and affection from you, and it seems to me, all for no good reason. It sounds like you've had a lifetime of being a casualty or a victim in someone else's war, always under attack and never safe from harm. I think I would have found that an incredibly painful life to live. Right now I find it really painful to hear you talking about it. It is like I am really aware of you holding back all that pain that you won't allow yourself to feel.'

She nodded, quietly in affirmation, without speaking.

Gently and quietly, I went on to say, 'You've told me about all of these really painful experiences and yet, you still seem to talk about them rather like a news reporter talking about a battle in a far away country. It feels to me almost as though you've locked away all of your feelings, like there's a part of you that is here, but it is safely locked away so it can't get out and harm you?'

I paused and then continued gently, 'I guess I'm also wondering if you feel you need to protect me from those feelings too? Like you think your feelings are really dangerous for you and for me?'

She nodded quietly again.

I went on, 'I wonder what it would be like for you to allow your feelings to be here in this room, with me? I wonder what it would be like for you to be here with your whole self, feelings and all?'

She made no verbal response but just sat looking at me in an expressionless way. I noticed though, that she had sat up a little more in her chair and that she was gripping her hands together tightly and was twisting her wedding ring on her finger. Her feet had shot back under her chair and she seemed to be poised on her toes, almost as though she was ready to run away. I did not want to interpret this and at the same time it really felt to me like she was suddenly feeling very anxious or apprehensive and I got a strong feeling that she wanted to push me away. I also realised that I was suddenly feeling quite anxious too, as though something very frightening was about to happen – I suddenly felt like running away and ending the session.

In my rational mind, I knew I had nothing to be frightened of and realised that these feelings might be hers that I was picking up, rather than mine. It was very important, therefore, for me to be fully present in the room as myself and to own and acknowledge what I was experiencing. It was important for me to try to enable her to be present with her own feelings for herself.

So, again very gently, I said, 'I've suddenly begun to feel very anxious, nervous and kind of scared that something frightening is just about to happen to me. I know I don't have anything to be frightened of, so I'm wondering if I am picking up the feelings that you are having, that you don't feel able to tell me about? I've noticed how you seem to have become rather tense after what I was just saying and I'm wondering if what I said has made you feel anxious or nervous and wanting to leave?'

I continued, quietly saying, 'I'm not telling you that you must bring your feelings here. I'm just noticing that you don't seem to do that and letting you know that you could choose to do so, because it is safe enough to do that here. I'm OK if you're not ready to do that yet – and I'd really like you to choose to let me meet all the different parts of you, when you are ready. I also know that your feelings can't harm me, so you don't need to protect me from them.'

After a long silence, Linda said, with tears in her eyes and a slight tremor in her voice: 'No, I'm not ready yet.' I got a real sense that she was really in touch with her pain at that moment.

'That's OK,' I said. 'And I get a sense that you are really getting in touch with that pain right now.'

After another shorter silence she said: 'I want you to know, I've just realised that this is the first time anyone has been interested in my feelings. It felt like you were really here with me, rather than just sat there listening.'

She went on to say, 'I've been taught that it is not safe to show my feelings. If I do, I'll get punished for it. It's like my feelings are a part of me that nobody else has ever wanted to know.'

Over the next few months, Linda began to bring more and more of herself into the room and to be prepared to actually be there experiencing her feelings rather than just talking about them in an emotionless way. This led to her being much more able to be with her feelings outside the counselling room and to make very significant and positive changes in her life as she began to choose to value her feelings and to choose not to be abused.

This is an example of how being more therapeutically present was helpful for the client and also for me as the counsellor.

The whole self of the client

In his theory of personality and behaviour, as described in Chapter 1, Rogers suggested that in striving towards self-actualisation and becoming a fully functioning person, each individual reacts as an organised whole to their experiencing of their reality. The separate parts of the person do not operate individually, they work together to ensure the survival of the individual. For this reason, it is essential that the counsellor responds to the whole of the client's self. In the case of Linda, it was clear that at both a conscious and an unconscious level, she had organised herself so that the feeling part of herself could no longer be damaged in the way that it had been. She had worked hard to hide away the damaged, hurt, and frightened feeling part of herself so that she could survive in her marriage and in her work and other relationships. As her counsellor, it was important that I made it safe for her to allow that part of herself to be present and no longer hidden. It was essential that I really set out to be there with the whole of myself, in order to be able to be with the whole of Linda.

The whole self and 'cultural competence'

In bringing the whole of myself into a relationship with the whole self of my client, it is really important to reflect on and be aware of the various cultural differences there may be between us. It is essential, as a counsellor, to be fully aware of my own and my client's cultural and social and context. In using the term 'culture', I am of course doing so in its widest sense. What are all the contextual ways in which I and my client are different? The person-centred approach and, indeed, counselling itself have often been stereotyped as white, middle-class activities which have little to offer those from other ethnic or cultural backgrounds. In more recent years, particular attention has been given to improving equality of opportunities and valuing diversity in counselling. Most recently, attention has been turned towards the notion of cultural competence. Cultural competence refers to an ability to interact effectively with people of different cultures. Cultural competence comprises four components:

1 An awareness of one's own cultural worldview,
2 An awareness of one's own attitude towards cultural differences,
3 Knowledge of different cultural practices and worldviews, and
4 Cross-cultural skills.

Developing cultural competence results in an ability to understand, communicate with, and effectively interact with people across cultural differences (Martin and Vaughan, 2007). This is plainly about far more than equal opportunities and valuing difference, and seeks to build on those two concepts in an active way. Cultural competence is a developmental process that evolves over an extended period and is based on a defined set of values and principles. It demonstrates behaviours, attitudes, policies, and structures that enable organisations and the people in them to work effectively cross-culturally. In our widely diverse society, it is essential that counsellors are able to be culturally competent. For me, this applies to the work of developing an effective relationship with my clients, whatever cultural background they come from, and takes account of the various ways in which my client and I are different. For me, it is an essential element of my continuing professional development that I am continuing to work on improving my awareness and understanding of my social and cultural context and that of my clients. My work on this includes mixing and working with people from a wide variety of backgrounds, undertaking specific cultural competence training, reading widely and exploring it in supervision and in my own personal therapy.

The whole self and an ethical caution

In wanting to be present with my whole self, with my client, I want to make it clear that I am talking about my emotional and psychological self and not with aspects of my physical self. It is very much a personal view of mine that I need to be very careful in presenting and engaging with my physical self with my client, particularly in this current litigious day and age. As I have written above, I believe counselling to be a professional relationship. I equate my role to that of a doctor, a lawyer or a dentist, which are all governed by important ethical considerations. Would my doctor or my lawyer hug me if I was distressed? Would I try to hug them? How would they respond if I said I wanted to hug them? It seems to me that they would be pretty unlikely to do that. This has led me to believe that I need to be very cautious about the use of touch or physical contact in the counselling relationship. In supervision I have often been told by a supervisee that they have been very touched by their client's distress and wanted to reach out and physically comfort the client; or that their client had said that they wanted to hug the counsellor and the counsellor wanted to respond to that request by hugging the client. While I want to be very accepting of how my supervisee feels, I also want to challenge them to explore what this is about, in them. Whose needs would this hug be meeting? What psychological processes might be going on? What impacts will this have on the therapeutic relationship? What might happen as a consequence? What might they be tempted or asked to do next? While I would not suggest that counsellors should never touch or hug their clients, I do feel that we should be very cautious about doing that. As a counsellor, I am not there to make my clients feel better, I am there to help them to understand and deal more effectively with their own feelings. And I must always take responsibility for dealing with my own feelings.

At an important theoretical level, when we are entering, through relational depth, into our client's world of feelings with our empathy, we need to remember Rogers' view of the importance of retaining the 'as-if' quality (Rogers, 1980: 140). We should never actually be in our client's world, becoming enmeshed in their feelings. In a paradoxical way, we need to develop the capacity to be both close and separate at the same time. We need to remember that this is a professional relationship with an ethical responsibility to maintain clear boundaries.

While I want to be experienced by my client as warm and understanding, I also want them to know that I am providing a safe and contained space, which they can trust me not to abuse in order to meet my needs, or indeed in order not to rescue them from learning to cope with their feelings. In order to maintain this paradoxical relationship of being close and separate, I like to retain what I have come to think of as a '*clinical distance*' between my client and myself. This distance can and will vary from client to client. However, for me, it will always be there and will always exemplify the difference between a personal relationship and a professional relationship. I believe all counsellors, whatever their modality, have a clear ethical responsibility to ensure that differentiation between the two kinds of relationship is always in place. I believe that this is particularly important for person-centred counsellors, for whom engaging in a warm and intimate relationship with clients is an essential aspect of our practice.

Transparency and self-disclosure – another ethical consideration

In Chapter 4, I described an experience of deep psychological contact with my client James, in which I said that one of the keys to establishing psychological contact was being prepared to take the risk of being transparent with my feelings in the moment to my client. It is ethically important to differentiate between self-disclosure and being transparent.

Self-disclosure is when the counsellor discloses their 'story' about the things that have happened to them, or talking about past or current events in their life. At its worst, this becomes the game of 'Me too'. It also runs the risk of causing the client to want to look after the counsellor and might lead to them changing roles. All counsellors, whatever their modality, should keep self-disclosure to an absolute minimum and should only disclose something if it is clear it would be helpful to the client and the relationship. For example, in working with a client who is seriously ill, it may be helpful to say that I have had my experience of serious illness and the impact that had on me, without going into any detail. Similarly, working with a client who has experienced a significant bereavement, it may be helpful to disclose that I have had a significant loss and am aware of the effect that had on me, again without going into any details. Clients can often come with the mythological belief that their counsellor is really 'sorted', really 'together' and has never had any real problems, and it can be very helpful to know that their counsellor has a real understanding of what they are experiencing.

Transparency is really specific to the person-centred approach as an aspect of authenticity, genuineness, or being real. It is the capacity of the counsellor to be present in the moment with their feelings, in a way that is appropriate and helpful to the client, in the relationship. I am using 'appropriate' in two senses. First, transparency needs to be appropriate in relation to the depth to which I am transparent with my feelings; and secondly, it needs to be appropriate in terms of timeliness. I have learned to trust my intuition and to be prepared to take the risk of being transparent with my feelings in the relationship with my clients and also in my everyday life. In counselling, I have learned that if I have a feeling in the moment in that relationship, I need to err on the side of expressing it. After all, it is my feeling and it is important that I value my feelings and take the risk of expressing them. Not least, this will model for the client a different way of being that they may choose to try for themselves.

A living, growing theory and practice

Carl Rogers never intended that the person-centred approach should become a set of inflexible rules about how counselling should be practised. Neither did he intend that his theory should be seen as some form of unchallengeable dogma. He always presented his theories as a hypothesis of what might be true. He tentatively suggested his theories as a proposed explanation made in the light of his own experience, which he intended should be used as a basis for further investigation. He was clearly committed to the notion that his ideas should be the starting point for new ideas and further development, ideally tested out through rigorous research.

He was clearly opposed to the person-centred approach standing still and strongly supported its continuing growth as a living, developing theory and practice. I am sure he would have been both flattered and intrigued to see the developments which have taken place since he died in 1985, leading to the appearance of what Pete Sanders calls 'the schools of therapy related to the person-centred approach' (Sanders, 2004).

My original training was in the person-centred approach, with a strong focus on the importance of the therapeutic relationship and a humanistic philosophical belief in the positive nature and the potential of all human beings. I have an unshakeable belief in: the actualising tendency, the six necessary and sufficient conditions, maintaining a non-expert stance and a non-directive attitude, striving to be phenomenological, avoiding interpretation and a real dislike of the use of techniques. In the past, some have described this as a 'purist' approach. That description has never sat comfortably with me, as it seems to imply that there is a pure or true way of being person-centred, which seems so at odds with what Rogers himself believed. I would rather describe my approach as 'orthodox', which recognises my commitment to his original ideas and values, but acknowledges the changes that have occurred in the ways that I work, as a result of my learning from my own experience and the experience of others.

Rogers himself recognised that even for him there was no one way of working. What was important was that he stayed true to the general principles that he believed in, rather than working to a set of rules. After all, he was fully committed to the person-centred approach, as a way of being rather than a way of doing.

The importance of trusting in your intuition

Another way in which Rogers indicated his belief that the person-centred approach should not be locked into a set of rigid procedures and techniques is demonstrated in his writing about the importance of trusting in his intuition, recognising that when he did this he might find himself working in quite unexpected ways. At the start of this chapter, I quoted from Rogers' statement that whenever he was closest to his inner, intuitive self, then whatever he did seemed to be full of healing. Trusting in your intuition can be a risky and quite scary thing to do, especially when we are transfixed by the fear of being complained against. I guess that in the early stages of becoming a person-centred counsellor, it can be quite difficult to trust in your intuition. It's a bit like learning to drive a car. In the early stages we have to learn to do it in a mainly mechanistic way, almost 'doing it by numbers'. It takes a lot of practice and a lot of learning by making mistakes to become a fluent, confident driver. That is true also for becoming a counsellor, and it is important to be prepared to take the risk of trusting in your intuition and really relaxing into the relationship with each client. If we make mistakes, we can always own those and apologise – and sometimes those mistakes actually work to advantage.

I remember working with a client, whom I will call Trudy, where that happened for me. She was in her early forties, very tall and very slim, always immaculately turned out. She came from a very middle-class background, was a regular church-goer and hated the use of swear words. Her presenting problems were in relation to recurrent phases of anorexia and her apparent complete inability to maintain an effective, intimate relationship. We had been working together for about six months and had developed a good therapeutic relationship. One day she walked into my consulting room, closing the door behind her. As she turned around, she had her hand up covering her mouth. From behind her hand she said:

'I'm sorry about this. I've just been for my Botox injection. Of course, I don't care at all about how I look!'

My immediate, intuitive response was a rather forceful: 'Oh, bollocks', at which she looked rather startled.

I immediately started to apologise saying, 'Perhaps I shouldn't have said that, or at least not sworn.'

As she sat down in her chair she said, 'Mm perhaps you shouldn't have, but you did get through to me in a way you haven't done before. Your reaction was really genuine, like you knew what I said was totally false and I really heard that. I guess I need to stop pretending and really start to try to be me.'

At the moment after I had said it, it felt like a really crass mistake, particularly knowing her aversion to swearing – and yet it worked to both our advantages as we went on to explore how we could be more real with each other in our sessions and how she could be more real in her outside worlds.

At a theoretical level, it seems to me an example of where it was more important for me to be completely and intuitively genuine and to communicate that, rather than focusing on being accepting and/or empathic. Strangely, my genuineness seemed also to be experienced as really having an empathic sense of how false she really felt.

Each client is a new venture in relating

I began this chapter with Carl Rogers' words about the importance of presence in the counselling relationship. I will end it with this further quotation, which could be considered to be among the most powerful words that Carl Rogers wrote:

> To the therapist, it is a new venture in relating, each time she meets a new client. She feels, 'Here is this other person, my client, I'm a little afraid of him, afraid of the depths in him as I am a little afraid of the depths in myself. Yet as he speaks, I begin to feel a little respect for him, to feel my kinship to him. I sense how frightening his world is for him, how tightly he tries to hold it in place. I would like to sense his feelings, and I would like him to know that I understand his feelings. I would like him to know that I can stand with him in his tight, con-stricted little world, and that I can look upon it relatively unafraid. Perhaps I can make it a safer world for him. I would like my feelings in this relationship with him to be as clear and transparent as possible, so that they are a discernible reality for him, to which he can return again and again. I would like to go with him on the fearful journey into himself, into the buried fear, and hate, and love which he has never been able to let flow in him. I recognise that this is a very human and unpredictable journey for me as well as for him, and that

I may, without even knowing my fear, shrink away within myself, from some of the feelings he discovers. To this extent I know I will be limited in my ability to help him. I realise that at times his own fears may make him perceive me as uncaring, as rejecting, as an intruder, as one who does not understand. I want fully to accept these feelings in him, and yet I hope also that my own real feelings will show through so clearly that in time he cannot fail to perceive them. Most of all I want him to encounter in me a real person. I do not need to be uneasy as to whether my own feelings are 'therapeutic'. What I am and what I feel are good enough to be a basis for therapy, if I can transparently **be** what I am and what I feel in relationship to him. Then perhaps he can be what he is, openly and without fear. (Rogers, 1961: 66–7)

This is how I would like it to be in my relationships with my clients. That my very presence is therapeutic and can make it safe for my client to be present with their whole self, in order to discover how they can be different – and to enable them to choose to do that, in order to become more fully functioning. I would also like to be experienced in that way in my everyday life, that it is truly my way of being. It is perhaps also important for me to refer to what I have said above about my belief that there is no one way of being person-centred. This book is very much my own, personal take on person-centred philosophy, theory and practice, as I have experienced it, developed it, practised it as a therapist and lived it in all aspects of my mature adult life.

Recommended reading

Mearns, D. (1994) *Developing Person-centred Counselling*. London: Sage.

Thorne, B. (1992) *Carl Rogers*. London: Sage.

Rogers, Carl R. (1961) *On Becoming a Person*. London: Constable.

Rogers, Carl R. (1980) *A Way of Being*. New York: Houghton Mifflin.

Sanders, P. (ed.) (2004) *The Tribes of the Person-centred Approach: an Introduction to the Schools of Therapy Related to the Person-centred Approach*. Ross-on-Wye: PCCS Books.

Bozarth, J. (1998) *Person-centred Therapy: a Revolutionary Paradigm*. Ross-on-Wye: PCCS Books.

Cooper, M., O'Hara, M., Schmid, P.F. and Wyatt, G. (eds) (2007) *The Handbook of Person-centred Psychotherapy and Counselling*. Basingstoke: Palgrave Macmillan.

References

BACP (2010) *Ethical Framework for Good Practice in Counselling and Psychotherapy* (Revised Edition). Leicestershire: BACP.

Berenson, B.G. and Carkhuff, R.R. (1967) *Sources of Gain in Counselling and Psychotherapy: Readings and Commentary.* New York: Holf, Rinehart & Winston.

Casemore, R., Dryden, W. and Jacobs, M. (2002) *It Ain't Necessarily So – On the Role of Congruence, Authenticity and Appropriate Transparency in the Therapeutic Encounter.* University of Warwick Centre for Life Long Learning.

Cooper, M. (2008a) *Essential Research Findings in Counselling & Psychotherapy: The Facts are Friendly.* Lutterworth: BACP and Sage.

Cooper, M. (2008b) 'The facts are friendly', *Therapy Today,* 19(7): 12.

Dru, A. ([1938] 1967) *Introduction to the Journals of Kierkegaard.* London: Fontana. (Originally published in 1938, Oxford: Oxford University Press.)

Geller, S. and Greenberg, L. (2002) 'Therapeutic presence: therapist's experience of presence in the therapeutic encounter', *Person-Centred and Experiential Psychotherapies* (Vol. 1). Ross-on-Wye: PCCS Books.

Goldstein, K. (1939) *The Organism.* New York: American Book Co.

Kirschenbaum, H. and Henderson, V.L. (eds) (1990) *The Carl Rogers Reader.* London: Constable.

Koch, S. (ed.) (1959) *Psychology: a Study of Science* (7 Vols). New York: McGraw-Hill.

Leitaur, G. (1993) 'Authenticity, congruence and transparency', in D. Brazier (ed.), *Beyond Carl Rogers.* London: Constable.

Martin, M. and Vaughan, B. (2007) 'The Nuts and Bolts of Diversity and Inclusion', *Strategic Diversity and Inclusion Management,* 1(1): 31–6.

Maslow, A.H. (1943) 'A theory of human motivation', *Psychological Review*, 50: 370–96.

Mearns, D. (1994) *Developing Person-centred Counselling*. London: Sage.

Prouty, G. (1994) *Theoretical Evolutions in Person-centred/Experiential Therapy: Applications to Schizophrenic and Retarded Psychoses*. London: Praeger.

Patterson, C.H. and Watkins, C.E. (1996) *Theories of Psychotherapy* (5th edn). New York: Harper Collins.

Rogers, Carl R. (1942) *Counselling and Psychotherapy: Newer Concepts in Practice*. New York: Houghton Mifflin.

Rogers, Carl R. (1979) *Client Centred Therapy: Its Current Practice, Implications and Theory*. London: Constable.

Rogers, Carl R. (1957) 'The necessary and sufficient conditions of psychological personality change', *Journal of Consulting Psychology*, 21(2): 95–103.

Rogers, Carl R. (1959) 'A theory of therapy, personality and interpersonal relationships as developed in the client centre framework', in S. Koch (ed.), *Psychology: a Study of Science, Volume 3: Formulations of the Person and the Social Context*. New York: McGraw-Hill, pp. 184–256.

Rogers, Carl R. (1961) *On Becoming a Person: a Therapist's View of Psychotherapy*. New York: Houghton Mifflin.

Rogers, Carl R. (1967) 'The interpersonal relationship in the facilitation of learning', in H. Kirschenbaum and V.L. Henderson (eds) (1990), *The Carl Rogers Reader*. London: Constable.

Rogers, Carl R. (1970) *Encounter Groups*. New York: Harper & Row.

Rogers, Carl R. (1980) *A Way of Being*. New York: Houghton Mifflin.

Rogers, Carl R. (1986) 'Reflection of feelings', *Person-Centred Review*, 1(4): 375–7.

Rogers, Carl R. (1987) 'Client-centered? Person-centered?', *Person-Centered Review*, 2(1): 11–13.

Rogers, Carl R. and Freiberg, H.J. (1994) *Freedom to Learn* (revised 3rd edn). Oxford: Maxwell MacMillan International.

Sanders, P. (ed.) (2004) *The Tribes of the Person-centred Approach: an Introduction to the Schools of Therapy Related to the Person-centred Approach.* Ross-on-Wye: PCCS Books.

Schön, D.A. (1971) *Beyond the Stable State.* London: Temple Smith.

Thorne, B. (1992) *Carl Rogers.* London: Sage.

The following is a list of useful websites about Carl Rogers and the Person-Centred Approach:

Carl Rogers.info: www.carlrogers.info/index.html

The Carl Rogers info website serves as a gateway to the work of Dr Carl Rogers and the many disciplines he influenced. Its primary audience is scholars and practitioners. It is a project of Saybrook Graduate School and Research Center, funded by the proceeds of the 2002 Carl R. Rogers Centennial Symposium.

The site includes a bibliography of books and articles by and about Rogers and the Person-Centered Approach (PCA) with links to those that are available online. It makes available a collection of rich media – selected audio and video archives that are streamed as Windows Media, as well as samples from the CD ROM *Carl Rogers: A Daughter's Tribute* and Howard Kirschenbaum's videotape *Carl Rogers and the Person-Centered Approach.* The audio collection is selected from the Carl R. Rogers archive at University of California at Santa Barbara. A comprehensive list of (and links to) worldwide organisations and training centres connected with Rogers and the Person-Centered Approach is included.

British Association for the Person-Centred Approach: www.bacp. co.uk

The site for the organisation that promotes and supports the Person-Centred Approach in the UK. Find local groups and events, such as conferences. Membership is available.

The World Association for Person-Centred and Experiential Psychology and Counselling: www.pce-world.org/

Provides a worldwide forum for practitioners and scholars working within the person-centred and the experiential paradigms. Fosters the exchange of research, theory and practice across language groups and cultures. Supports and encourages scientific study as well as improvement of practice in the field of psychotherapy and counselling. Promotes person-centred and experiential perspectives, and stimulates cooperation and dialogue with other psychotherapeutic orientations.

Natalie Rogers' site:www.nrogers.com/carlrogersbooks.html

Link to pages on Natalie Rogers' site (Carl Rogers' daughter) about her father. Biography, books, life events and more about Carl Rogers.

PCCS Books: www.pccs-books.co.uk/index.php

PCCS is a small publishing company specialising in books on counselling and psychotherapy with a focus on the person-centred approach and critical psychology. This is a great site for person-centred books and journals.

Allan Turner's site: www.allanturner.co.uk/

A wide collection of person/client-centred material. Many links to further PCA sites, including associations, books, a directory of counsellors, events, jobs, training, videos, etc.

Index